# Essential
# Scottish
## Cookery

# Essential Scottish Cookery

Classic recipes from the Scottish kitchen

Carol Wilson and Christopher Trotter

**BLACK & WHITE PUBLISHING**

This edition published in 2009 by Black & White Publishing Ltd
29 Ocean Drive, Edinburgh EH6 6JL

Produced by Anness Publishing Limited
Hermes House, 88–89 Blackfriars Road, London, SE1 8HA

10 9 8 7 6 5 4 3 2    09 10

ISBN: 978-1-84502-186-3

Printed in Singapore

**Publisher's Acknowledgements**
All pictures © Anness Publishing Ltd, except where the publisher would like
to thank the following picture agencies for use of their images:
Glenfiddich: p34 (top), and p35 (bottom). Glenmorangie: p10 (top),
p12 (bottom). MacSween of Edinburgh: p19 (bottom).
Scottish Viewpoint: p8 (bottom).

Previously published as part of a larger volume, *Scottish Heritage Food
and Cooking*

Printed in Singapore

**Notes**: Bracketed terms are intended for American readers.
For all recipes, quantities are given in both metric and imperial measures and,
where appropriate, measures are also given in standard cups and spoons.
Follow one set, but not a mixture, because they are not interchangeable.
Standard spoon and cup measures are level.
1 tsp = 5ml, 1 tbsp = 15ml, 1 cup = 250ml/8fl oz
Australian standard tablespoons are 20ml. Australian readers should use 3 tsp in
place of 1 tbsp for measuring small quantities of gelatine, flour, salt etc.
Medium (US large) eggs are used unless otherwise stated.

**Nutritional information**: The nutritional analysis given for each recipe is
calculated per portion (i.e. serving or item), unless otherwise stated. If the recipe
gives a range, such as Serves 4–6, then the nutritional analysis will be for the
smaller portion size, i.e. 6 servings. Measurements for sodium do not include salt
added to taste.

# Contents

# The Scottish kitchen

The Scots take great pride in their cuisine, and hospitality
has always been a tradition. They prefer to use local produce,
and are fortunate in the plentiful supplies of meat, game,
fish and shellfish, fruit and vegetables, dairy and cereal crops
that Scotland provides. All the recipes featured here are easy
to prepare and have been grouped into six chapters to
make selecting the right dish easy.
The Scots are careful to preserve their time-honoured heritage
produce and dishes. Aberdeen Angus beef, Highland game,
Tayside berries, salmon and other fish and shellfish and of
course Scotch whisky are recognized as the finest in the world,
and this book will show you how to recreate classic Scottish
dishes using these delicious ingredients.

# Fresh fish

Scotland is home to an ancient fishing tradition, its busy fishing ports ranging all along the coastline and the Islands. The natural harbours along the east coast have produced a thriving fishing industry. On the west coast, fishing gradually developed after people lost their lands and sought sustenance from the sea. On the Islands, fishing was a way of life. A plentiful supply of fish, especially smoked and cured fish, has always been the country's traditional heritage ever since the days when slow travel made the preservation of fish an economic necessity.

Preserving fish from the earliest times was achieved by wind drying (*blawn*) or sun drying (*rizzared* or *tiled*), pickling or smoking, according to the type of fish. Oily fish, such as herring and mackerel, were more problematic and it wasn't until the 14th century that a way to preserve oily fish was devised by a

**Above** *Salmon steaks contain the bone and so are ideal for poaching, grilling (broiling) or adding to fish soups.*

Dutch man called William Beukelsz. The fish had to be freshly caught, gutted and rinsed, then packed tightly in barrels, layered with coarse salt to exclude air.

Entire families were involved in the business of fishing. Children collected and prepared bait and boys went to sea with their fathers when they were 14 years old. Fishing communities were closely knit and boys married girls from

**Above** *Salmon fillets are the preferred cut for restaurants as they contain no bones and less fat and can be accompanied by fine sauces.*

their own or a nearby fishing village. The men went to sea, an arduous occupation at the best of times, but made even more exhausting and dangerous by the occasional storms, fogs and freezing-cold weather. The women baited the lines, gutted, cleaned and cured or smoked the fish and also sold the catch – often walking some distance to the nearest town with heavy *creels* (baskets) on their backs.

All types of fish were sold by fishwives, who went from door to door in rural areas. An old Edinburgh street cry was: "Haddies, caller haddies, fresh an' loupin' in the creel", advertising live haddock flapping in their baskets.

## Types of fish

The fish enjoyed today are different from those eaten in the past. Sadly, some fish are less common now. On the other hand, fish farming has led to a greater availability of some fish, such as rainbow trout.

**Salmon** is the fish most often associated with Scotland. There are traditionally two main types of salmon, the Atlantic salmon from the sea and the wild salmon from the rivers. In addition there is now farmed salmon of

**Left** *Pittenweem in East Neuk remains an active fishing port, with a fish market at 8am every morning held in sheds on the harbourside.*

various qualities. These all have different flavours, colours and textures, with wild salmon being the finest.

**Herring** used to be plentiful and cheap, taking pride of place in Scottish fish cooking. The "silver darlings", as they were known, swam in huge shoals in Scottish seas, but once caught they had to be eaten as fresh as possible as they deteriorated quickly.

Plump and succulent with a rich flavour, they were cooked in various ways. A favourite dish throughout Scotland was Tatties and Herring, where the fish were steamed over the almost-cooked potatoes. Enormous quantities of salt-pickled herring were exported in barrels to Scandinavia and Russia (where they were a staple of the diet) in the 19th century.

Tasty, nutritious and easy to digest, herrings can be coated with rolled oats and fried in oil for a few minutes or simply grilled (broiled). They can be bought fresh or smoked and also pickled in spiced brine from delicatessen counters in supermarkets.

**Mackerel** is still caught abundantly around the coast, especially by small fishermen or locals fishing over the weekend. The mackerel are eaten as fresh as possible, usually simply pan-fried or grilled (broiled).

**Haddock** is now the most popular white fish in Scotland, often found in fish and chip shops. In the past it was preserved by salt-curing, and this was mentioned in the Household Book of James VI in the 16th century. It is used to make the ever-popular fish and chips, known as a "fish supper" in Scotland. Haddock is also delicious baked or steamed as well as coated in breadcrumbs or batter and fried. Many experienced fishmongers believe that very fresh fish is not always the best choice, and that it should be left for a while before cutting – the actual time depends on the type of fish. This is best left to the expert.

**Cod** is now an expensive fish, a result of overfishing in the Atlantic. It remains popular, often as a result of the many recipes and traditions surrounding it.

**Sea bass** is a flavourful fish with a fine soft texture, a favourite of the fish restaurants. Most is farmed these days as it is increasingly rare in the wild.

*Above*
*Sea trout is a rare delicacy enjoyed in Scotland's top restaurants.*

**Monkfish** used to be thrown back off the fishing boats, but are now prized fish both in the home and on the restaurant menu. The meaty tails are served with simple sauces.

**Trout** Rainbow trout is now enjoyed much more widely owing to new farms that have sprung up in the lochs and around the coastlines. Both fresh and smoked trout is exported abroad.

Sea trout and river (brown) trout are harder to come by these days and are rarely seen except on the occasional restaurant menu or, of course, if you catch one yourself.

*Above Mackerel are found in abundance around the coasts, and can often be bought fresh at the harbour.*

*Above Herring are especially popular on Shetland and the Orkneys owing to the Scandinavian influence.*

*Above Rainbow trout (top) are now farmed, while the river (brown) trout (bottom) can only be caught wild.*

# Smoked fish

In the days before refrigeration and fast transport, a major concern was the preservation of fish. They were smoked in home chimneys, over peat fires or in specially built sheds over halved whisky barrels. Today fish are generally smoked for flavour. Haddock, mackerel, sprats and herring are smoked over oak, beech, hickory, cherry wood, Douglas fir or whisky barrel chippings, which all produce a magnificent flavour. Every curer has his own unique brining recipe and secret flavourings.

Early Scandinavian settlers brought with them their tradition of hot-smoking fish, and it has continued to the present day. In the early 18th century the people of the tiny village of Auchmithie took their skills to the growing port of Arbroath, just north of Dundee and it became a centre for smoking. The salty, smoky, mellow aromas still waft enticingly through the town. Originally the fishwives arranged the fish on rods and smoked them over discarded whisky barrels, which produced a darker colour than those of today. The name "Arbroath smokie" is protected and can now only be used to describe haddock smoked in the traditional manner (dating back to the late 1800s) within an 8km/5-mile radius of Arbroath.

## Smoked haddock

Smoking haddock was a particular skill of the village of Findon (pronounced Finnan), south of Aberdeen, and it was from this village that the cure took its name. Pale golden Finnan haddock is renowned throughout the world and has a superb delicate flavour.

The original cures produced a hard, heavily smoked fish, but modern cures have improved the flavour and texture enormously. There are hot-smoked and cold-smoked cures, with several regional variations.

Pales or Glasgow pales have a shorter brining and smoking time than Finnan haddock. Some are very lightly smoked and thus have only a slight smoky flavour and just a hint of colour. They are usually made from smaller fish. Smoked fillet, sometimes known as Aberdeen fillet, is a single fillet from a large haddock. The skin is left on to hold the fish together during the curing process. Golden Cutlet is made from a fillet of haddock or whiting with the skin removed. It is only lightly brined and smoked so has less flavour than any other cure.

The garish yellow dyed smoked haddock are best avoided. You'll find authentic Finnan haddock at good

*Above Quality fish and shellfish for smoking is farmed in Loch Fyne.*

fishmongers. It is delicious simmered gently in milk or water and served with a poached egg on top. Smoked haddock is an essential ingredient of Cullen skink, a creamy fish and potato soup. Hot-smoked haddock or Arbroath smokies are also known by their original names, *tied tailies* or *pinwiddies*, and are succulently moist with a wonderful flavour. Whole haddock are split open and the head and guts removed before they are tied in pairs by their tails, then lightly brined and smoked over oak or beech wood until cooked.

*Above Smoked haddock is a favourite for breakfast dishes, including smoked haddock topped with poached eggs.*

*Above Arbroath smokies are hot-smoked haddock that are left whole and always sold in pairs.*

*Above Smoked halibut has a translucent white flesh and lovely delicate flavour.*

**Above**
*Kippers are
smoked over
an oak fire for
4–18 hours.*

### Kippers and smoked herrings

Freshly caught herrings were originally dried over smoking seaweed and sprinkled with saltwater to preserve them. Kippers are plump herring that have been split, cleaned and soaked in brine for a few minutes then hot smoked. Scottish fishwives travelled to the villages of Craster (known as the kipper capital of England) and Seahouses in England in the 19th century to gut the herring ready for smoking. They lived in dilapidated buildings, known as kip houses, which were only suitable for sleeping in – hence the British slang term "having a kip". Those from Loch Fyne are smoked over oak chips (often from whisky barrels) and are particularly good. They can be grilled (broiled), baked or simmered in boiling water. An old way of cooking them was to place the kippers in a jug of boiling hot water and leave them for 4–5 minutes, by which time they were cooked.

Bloaters are whole herring that have been cured and lightly smoked, but not split or gutted. The name may come from the Old Norse *blautr*, or from the fact that the fish are plumper than dry-cured fish. They have a delicate smoky flavour and remain silver in colour. They were popular in the 19th century.

### Other smoked fish

Almost every type of fish in Scotland has a tradition of being smoked, with lesser or greater success. Smoked salmon is without doubt the best-known type.

**Above**
*Smoked mackerel
makes a tasty
pâté.*

**Smoked trout** is a favourite for making delicious patés and mousses and fine first courses, often served with dill or horseradish sauce. The best is first brined and then gutted and smoked over birch with a little peat for a smokier flavour. High-quality smoked trout is now prepared in a similar way to smoked salmon.

**Smoked mackerel** has a rich flavour and a succulent velvety-smooth texture. It can be eaten cold with a salad and makes a delicious pâté.

**Smoked halibut** has a translucent white flesh and a delicate smoky flavour. It is smoked and thinly sliced in a similar way to smoked salmon.

**Above** *Smoked trout fillets make an excellent first course.*

**Right** *Sea trout is relatively rare now, so smoked sea trout is a real treat.*

# Fresh shellfish

The Scots have always made the most of their superb shellfish and have devised many creative recipes for them. The vast Scottish waters provide rich feeding grounds and yield some of the world's best shellfish.

### Crustaceans

These curious-looking creatures with 10 legs make for some delicious dishes. Available around the coast, they are often exported to restaurants around Europe.

**Lobster** is regarded as one of the tastiest shellfish and has a rich, intense flavour. Originally eaten by the poor, it became a gourmet food in the 19th century. They are thought to be at their best in August. Lobster is usually boiled but can also be grilled (broiled). The dark blue-green shell becomes scarlet when cooked. Lobsters and crabs were originally fished by coaxing them from the rocks with a stick. In the 1750s creel fishing was introduced, using special pots fitted with bait. By the end of the 18th century catches, particularly in Orkney, were enormous.

***Above***
*Langoustines are now a speciality of many top restaurants.*

**Langoustines** are also known as Dublin Bay prawns (jumbo shrimp), Norway lobsters or crayfish. They were largely regarded as a nuisance by fishermen until the 1960s when increased foreign travel began to create a demand for them. As scampi they became a gourmet food, exported all

over the world and a fixture on restaurant menus. Pale orange-pink with white striped claws, they are sold fresh or pre-boiled and may be eaten hot or cold. If fresh, boil in salted water for 3–4 minutes and serve in the shell. Pull off the head and claws, cut through the cartilage underneath and open out. Remove the whole tail and take out the spinal cord. Crack the claws and remove the tasty meat.

**Crabs**, or *partans* as they are called in Scotland, are caught in creels and are sold live or pre-boiled. There are two main types: the common brown crab or the rarer shore variety. Their reddish-brown shells are tinged with purple and the claws are black. The flavour of the white meat is more delicate than lobster and connoisseurs regard Scottish crabs as superior to English crabs. The cooked meat is removed from the shell and claws and should be eaten as fresh as possible. *Partan bree*, a creamy crab soup, is a famous Scottish dish.

***Above*** *The brown or common crab is easy to come by along the coast. It makes an excellent dressed crab.*

***Left*** *Oyster beds on Loch Fyne provide the market with succulent, well-flavoured farmed oysters.*

***Above*** *Razor clams must be cleaned thoroughly before cooking. They are collected from the island beaches.*

***Above*** *Clams were a dietary mainstay in the past. They were collected from beaches and coastlines.*

***Above*** *Native oysters are slow-growers and are considered the finest oysters. They are also the most expensive.*

## Molluscs

Many of these small shelled creatures can simply be collected from the beaches or coastlines around Scotland, making them an excellent free food source for locals. Cockles (small clams), clams and razor clams fall easily into this category, although they are more difficult to find these days for sale.

**Oysters** were once so plentiful that they were a staple of the poor and were included in many dishes to eke out the ingredients. They were eaten alone, used as a stuffing for fish or meat and made into sauces. Native oyster beds were overfished, became polluted and, by the middle of the 20th century, were almost wiped out. Oyster farming in the unpolluted waters of sea lochs on the west coast and around the Islands has brought about a revival. The Pacific oyster is often used for farming and is more elongated than the native oyster. To open an oyster, hold it in one hand, well wrapped in a dish towel. Push the point of an oyster knife into the oyster's hinge and apply pressure, and retain the liquor. You could ask your fishmonger to do this. Serve on a plate of crushed ice with lemon wedges, brown bread and a sprinkling of cayenne pepper.

**Scallops** There are two types of scallops in Scotland – the Great scallop and the Queen scallop. The creamy white flesh is firm with a mild flavour and is enclosed in a shell that can measure up to 15cm/6in long. The orange coral is edible and has a rich flavour and smooth texture. Scallops need only a few minutes' cooking. It is important not to overcook them as the meat will become tough and rubbery, losing its sweet taste.

Scallops are also available still in their closed shells, when they are at their optimum freshness. To prepare them, scrub the shells well and place them curved side down in a low oven for a few minutes. Open the shells with a knife and wash under cold running water, then remove the grey-brown frill and the black intestine. Soak the flesh in iced water for several hours before using so the flesh becomes firm. Prick the coral with a needle before cooking to prevent it bursting. Serve the scallops in their shells.

**Mussels** make a wonderful main dish or first course. Musselburgh, near Edinburgh, was so named because of the large mussel bed at the mouth of the River Esk. It became a great mussel-eating centre.

Mussels (*Mytilus eduilis*) are commercially farmed, mainly along the west coast. They have less flavour and paler flesh than the wild, deep orange-fleshed mussels. Larger horse mussels (*Modiolus modiolus*) are known as *clabbie dubhs* in Scotland (from the Gaelic *clab-dubh*, meaning large black mouth) and have a robust flavour. Mussels must have tightly closed shells; discard any that remain open when tapped (and any that stay closed once cooked) as this indicates that they are not live. Scrub the shells to remove any barnacles, remove the beards then wash in several changes of cold water. Steam or boil in white wine or water, or add to fish stews.

***Below*** *Great or king scallops have a lovely sweet taste and delicate texture.*

# Game's rich flavours

Scotland's wild open country has long been home to a large variety of game, which has always had a place on Scottish meal tables, particularly in the Highlands and on the Islands. Game dealers and butchers sell game according to season, and the quality and flavour of Scottish game is unrivalled anywhere in the world.

Almost all game must be hung to develop flavour and tenderize the flesh. Birds are hung by the neck, unplucked, in a cool place. Deer are *gralloched* (gutted) and skinned before hanging. The length of time they are hung for depends on the type of game, where they are hung and the weather; game goes off quickly when it is thundery, for example.

Game is frequently cooked with the foods it lived on when alive. For example, rabbit is partnered with wild thyme and grouse with rowanberries or tiny raspberries. Any leftovers are made into soups and broths.

## Venison

Scottish venison is considered to be the best in the world and is one of the glories of Scottish cuisine. Red deer live in the wild hills and are the most common. The shooting season for stags is from 1 July to 20 October and for hinds from 21 October to 15 February. Stag meat has the fuller flavour of the two. Roe deer live in forests; the season for bucks is from 1 May to 20 October and for does from 21 October to 28 or 29 February. Fallow deer inhabit forests and parks and the season for bucks is from 1 August to 30 April and for does from 21 October to 15 February.

Farmed venison is less expensive than wild and the meat is more tender, with a delicate, less gamey flavour. Some deer farmers have developed a trade in venison sausages and pies. Wild venison is usually marinated in alcohol and oil to tenderize the flesh and keep it moist as it cooks. All venison is lean and low in cholesterol.

**Above** *The most common deer species in Scotland are the red deer and the roe deer. The male red deer are called stags and the females hinds. The roe deer are known as bucks and does.*

The age of the animal and the hanging time greatly affect the flavour and texture of the meat. Some deer are hung for only a few days, while others are hung for two weeks, by which time they have developed a high, strong gamey flavour.

The meat is dark red and close-grained with firm white fat. Most venison cuts should be cooked quickly and allowed to rest before serving, except shoulder and shin, which are better braised. The haunch, saddle or leg are best for roasting or for slicing into medallions. Chops from the ribs can be fried or grilled (broiled). A strong-flavoured meat, venison needs to be matched with robust flavours such as spices, rowanberries, juniper berries and red wine. The flank is best casseroled or minced (ground) and the neck is used in soups. The kidneys are usually fried. The liver is a great delicacy and can be fried or used (with the heart and flank) to make venison haggis.

**Above** *Venison cuts that benefit from long, slow cooking include neck (left), shoulder and shin. They make tasty stews and soups and are commonly used in pies.*

**Left** *Red deer haunch is a prime cut, ideal for roasting or making into steaks. It is now popular as a celebration spit roast, surrounded by roast vegetables and berries.*

*Above Rabbits are now farmed (top), although the wild rabbits (middle) are leaner and tastier. The saddle and leg joints (bottom) are the most frequently used.*

## Wild boar

A few enterprising Scottish farmers are producing wild boar – a very recent development that is proving popular with consumers. Unlike pork, wild boar is a red meat with a very tasty, slightly gamey flavour. It is similar to, but not as strong as, venison, and the taste becomes more pronounced as the animal ages. The meat is noted for its leanness and flavour and is sold fresh or processed into bacon and sausages. Prized cuts are the saddle and haunches, both of which can also be smoked to produce wild boar ham. Other cuts include loin, shoulder, loin chops, leg steaks and fillet (tenderloin).

## Hare and rabbit

A favourite catch in the Highlands, hare is hung for seven to ten days and the blood is reserved to enrich and thicken the gravy. Hares are at their best from October to January.

A well-hung hare would go into *bawd bree*, a traditional soup-stew that dates from the 16th century. *Bawd* is

the old Scots word for hare and *bree* means the juice or liquid in which food is cooked. Jugged hare, often served at harvest feasts, was made by packing a jointed hare into a large stone jar or jug with its blood, plus seasonings and spices. The jar was placed in a large pan of boiling water for about three hours until cooked.

Rabbits are best eaten fresh (although they can be hung), and wild rabbit has a stronger flavour. The meat tends to be dry so it should be well basted or cooked with liquid. Lowland Scots ate more rabbits than the Highlanders,

*Right Wild boar saddle (top) with fillet (tenderloin) and chops (bottom) can be treated like a good free-range pork.*

*Above Wild rabbits proliferate in all parts of Scotland, providing excellent game meat.*

and a favourite way of cooking them was with onions, or else they were simply roasted. Rabbit meat was also minced (ground) and mixed with pork and onions. This mixture was shaped into a roll and also used to make soups and pies. Kingdom of Fife pie is made with rabbit and pickled pork or bacon.

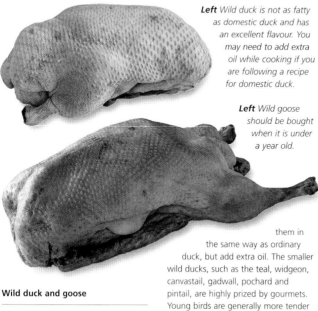

**Left** *Wild duck is not as fatty as domestic duck and has an excellent flavour. You may need to add extra oil while cooking if you are following a recipe for domestic duck.*

**Left** *Wild goose should be bought when it is under a year old.*

**Wild goose** makes a tasty roast. The plump Canada goose is the largest and most commonly found, although the smaller greylag, pinkfoot and whitefront are also good.

**Pheasant**

The diet of a pheasant does not include much heather because they do not frequent the high moorlands, so it has a mild flavour. If eaten without hanging their flavour is similar to that of chicken. After hanging, the flesh develops a mild gamey taste. The pheasant season extends from 1 October to 1 February, and they are at their best in November and December as the birds have more flavour after the first frosts. Pheasants are often bought as a brace (a cock and a hen bird). A cock usually weighs around 1.3kg/3lb and a hen about 900g/2lb. The hen is less dry than the

**Wild duck and goose**

Far less fatty than the domesticated birds, wild ducks and geese can still be found in Scotland. Try to get birds that come from inland waters, rather than from saltwater coasts and marshes as the flesh can tough and salty. It is also better to eat birds before they reach a year old.

**Wild ducks** Mallards are the largest and the most common wild ducks. Use them in the same way as ordinary duck, but add extra oil. The smaller wild ducks, such as the teal, widgeon, canvastail, gadwall, pochard and pintail, are highly prized by gourmets. Young birds are generally more tender and older ones can be tough and need to be cooked long and slow in a stew or casserole.

**Left** *Oven-ready cock (top) and hen pheasants can be bought from quality butchers. Although there are often small blemishes on the skin, pick a bird that looks plump and healthy.*

**Above** *Pheasants thrive in the Lowlands, and their meat is quite mildly flavoured. They are sold in pairs, a male (bottom) and a female, known as a brace. The hen is more tender and smaller than the cock and will serve three people, while the cock will serve four.*

cock and tends to have more flavour. They are grilled (broiled), roasted or jugged in the same way as hare, and are also good stuffed with apples.

### Grouse

The red grouse inhabits the Scottish moors where it feeds on heather, blueberries, grasses and herbs, which all impart a unique flavour to the flesh. The flavour varies according to the locality and the hanging time (usually two to seven days) and the meat is stronger than that of other grouse. They are shot from 12 August until 10 December. A native of Scotland, it is only found here and in the north of England.

Grouse flesh tends to be dry, and they were originally cooked on a spit so that they basted themselves as they turned. They can be split up the

backbone, spatchcocked, brushed with oil and grilled for 10–15 minutes. Grouse should be roasted quickly in a hot oven. Before roasting the bird can be stuffed with cranberries to keep it moist and complement the flavour. Wrap well in streaky (fatty) bacon or brush with butter and baste during cooking. After roasting, the legs (which have a bitter flavour) are usually removed and used in stews and soups where the long cooking mellows the bitterness. The Victorians often enjoyed cold roast grouse for breakfast.

### Partridge

The tasty partridge is making a comeback after many years of decline, thanks to the efforts of many estate owners and gamekeepers who have introduced both the French red-legged

***Above*** *Red-legged (left) and grey-legged partridges are two different species.*

partridge and the smaller native grey partridge. The shooting season is from 1 September to 1 February. Partridge develops more flavour if it is hung well. It can be casseroled or roasted, sometimes with an onion inside, or stuffed with wild mushrooms and cooked in the same way as grouse.

### Other game birds

**Woodcock** has a wonderfully rich flavour and is still found in many gaming reserves. It is roasted with berries and roasted root vegetables such as turnips and potatoes.
**Pigeons** are small and tasty, and are available all the year round, although each one provides only a small quantity of meat. Squab pigeons are the more tender young pigeons that have a good flavour and texture. They are now farmed commercially and good-quality pigeons are readily available from game butchers.

***Below*** *Wild pheasants can be found throughout Scotland and are easy and tasty game for locals and hunters.*

# Scotland's quality meats

From the lush pastures of the Lowlands to sheep-rearing in the bleak Highlands, Scotland's meats have the reputation for excellent flavour, high quality and natural rearing conditions.

Meat is enjoyed frequently in Scotland. In the past, a soup or stew would spread a few smaller joints around a whole family, and the innards would be made into haggis, black puddings (blood sausage) and delicious pie fillings.

***Above*** Tasty entrecôte (sirloin) steaks (top) are cut from the sirloin. The prime cut is the long, lean fillet (tenderloin) (bottom).

## Beef

Scottish beef from native breeds such as the shaggy, long-haired Highland cattle or the famous Aberdeen Angus – both of which tolerate the bleak, rugged terrain and harsh weather –

***Right*** Lamb leg and leg steaks are tender and good for roasting and barbecuing.

has achieved international renown for its superb rich full flavour and succulent texture.

Beef needs hanging to develop the flavour and tenderize the meat. Good-quality beef is dark red with a marbling of creamy coloured fat – bright red, wet-looking meat indicates that it has not been hung for long enough.

One of the oldest dishes using beef is Scotch collops, and the recipe appears in many old cookbooks. Originally the meat was thinly sliced, beaten with a rolling pin to flatten it, then seasoned with salt and pepper and fried quickly. "Scotching" meant cutting a criss-cross pattern on the meat before cooking.

Minced collops or "mince and tatties" is a much-loved dish. Minced (ground) beef is cooked very slowly with onions over a low heat until tender. Just before serving, a handful of toasted rolled oats is stirred in and the meat is served with baked or boiled potatoes. Properly made the dish is very tasty, but it is often ruined by the addition of water and cornflour (cornstarch) to thicken it.

Cold roast beef, left over from a roast joint, is often simmered with carrots in an onion gravy to make a dish known as *inky pinky*.

Cheaper, less tender cuts of beef, such as shin (shank), need long, slow cooking in liquid. Boiled beef is something of a misnomer, as the liquid should just bubble very gently for a few hours. Potted meat and meat loaves

are a speciality of Scottish cuisine and these can be bought at most butchers. Potted beef is called *potted hough*, the Scottish name for shin beef.

Forfar was an important centre of the beef trade in Angus, and a speciality of the town is Forfar Bridies, a type of pasty similar to a Cornish pasty. Filled with chopped rump (round) steak and onions, they were named after Maggie Bridie of Glamis, one of many people who sold the tasty pasties at local fairs and markets.

## Mutton and lamb

Mutton has been a favourite in Scotland for hundreds of years and in 19th-century Britain, Scottish mutton and lamb were renowned for their flavour and quality. Although sheep were reared mainly for milk and wool, they were slaughtered for meat, and often salted and preserved for winter.

Traditionally, every part of the animal was used – the shoulder and *gigot* (a French term for the leg) were braised or roasted; the blood was made into black pudding (blood sausage); the kidneys were fried; the heart, head and trotters were used in broth. Other parts went to make haggis. *Powsowdie* is a very old dish of sheep's head pie or broth.

There are many breeds of sheep in Scotland. Blackface sheep, for example, are a hardy breed that can withstand

*Below* Haggis is a traditional
Scottish dish.

the harshest of winters. They graze on heather-clad hills in summer and feed on hay and turnips in winter. Shetland sheep are a distinctive breed native to the Shetland Isles. The small sheep are very hardy and can weather severe conditions. Their diet of seaweed and heather, together with the salt carried on the strong winds to their pastures, gives them a unique, slightly gamey flavour, quite different from lamb derived from other breeds of sheep produced in other areas.

Salting mutton is still done in the Hebrides, Orkney, Shetland and some northern parts of the Highlands. In the Islands it is called *reested* or *reestit* mutton. The meat (sometimes cut up but always left on the bone) is cured with salt, sugar and spices (in the Highlands juniper berries are used) for up to three weeks, then hung to dry or smoked for 10 to 15 days. A small piece is sufficient to flavour a pot of soup or broth.

Traditional Scottish dishes such as Scotch broth needed long, slow cooking, as they used mutton from a mature sheep rather than young lamb as is more usual today. Mutton has a fuller, richer flavour and is gaining popularity once again, although it remains difficult to obtain.

Scotch pies, made with lamb, were originally sold in taverns and are now a national institution throughout Scotland. Mutton pies were praised by Dr Johnson on his tour of Scotland. The pies are sold by butchers and bakers and have a distinctive shape with a rim of pastry above the lid, which leaves a space that is often filled with mashed potatoes or baked beans. They are always eaten hot, never cold.

### Haggis and black pudding

Both a type of sausage that would have been a major part of the staple diet in centuries past, the haggis and the black pudding (blood sausage) have become great symbols of Scottish heritage, custom and tradition. They are still enjoyed widely today, although they are more frequently bought ready-made than prepared by hand in the home.

**Haggis** is actually a type of sausage, of which the outer cover is discarded and only the juicy inner meat is eaten. It is composed of mutton and lamb and their offal, highly spiced and bound together with oatmeal, and packed into a sheep's stomach ready for lengthy boiling. Nowadays haggis is generally sold cooked, ready for further cooking and reheating.

**Black pudding** is another quintessential Scottish food. It is a blood sausage that is usually highly spiced. It is bought already poached and is then sliced and fried for breakfast or supper, or to slip into a sandwich for a tasty lunch.

*Below* The nationalist poet Robert Burns immortalized the haggis in his memorable "Address to a haggis", which is recited throughout Scotland during the Burns Night celebrations.

# Dairy and cheese

Dairy products traditionally played an important role in providing nutrients and protein in the diet. As a result, cheese, butter, milk and cream abound in the old recipes, as well as many new ones too.

### Creams, milks and butter

Much of Scottish cooking is based on the flavourful addition of creams, milks or butter. Buttermilk, whey and sour milk were traditionally enjoyed as refreshing summer drinks, and buttermilk was added to mashed potatoes, porridge (oatmeal), scones and bannocks for extra flavour. In Shetland whey was fermented in oak casks for several months to produce *blaand*, a drink that has been revived and is now produced commercially.

Many traditional dishes are based on milk and cream, not only the creamy vegetables and mashed potatoes, but also the desserts and cakes. Cranachan

*Below Dairy farming is strong in the Lowlands, where luscious creams and tasty local cheeses are produced.*

*Below The wash for Bishop Kennedy includes a generous dash of whisky, giving a lovely tasty rind.*

is a delicious dessert traditionally made with fresh raspberries, oatmeal or porridge oats and fresh, thick cream. Many cakes and desserts were created with a large dollop of fresh cream in mind, such as the tarts and fruit pies and crumbles, or *frushies* as they are known. Cream and milk are also favourites in drinks, especially with whisky either as a cream liqueur or floating on top of a sumptuous Highland coffee.

Fresh flavoursome butter has been produced in Scotland for centuries. It is used in most cooked dishes, adding a rich taste. Bread, bannocks and fruit cakes are all spread liberally with soft pats of fresh butter at teatime.

### A wealth of cheeses

In the past there were a great many Scottish cheeses, some of which were made in the home. They were an important source of nourishment. Dairy industrialization led to a steep decline in farmhouse cheese-making. Happily there has been a resurgence of interest in traditional and speciality cheeses made by artisan cheese-makers across the country. Superb cheeses are still made by hand, using time-honoured methods. **Crowdie** is an ancient Highland cheese made from skimmed cow's milk and is similar to cottage cheese, with a sharp, acidic flavour. Uniquely Scottish, it was once used as part-payment of rent in the Highlands. After the Clearances

***Above*** *St Andrews is a Trappist-style washed-rind cheese from Perthshire.*

crowdie disappeared, but it was revived in the 1960s. It is unusual because it is half cooked. Fresh milk is left in a warm place to sour naturally, and then heated until it separates and curdles. The curds are hung up in a large square of muslin (cheesecloth) to drip. Some crowdie is mixed with double (heavy) cream before it is sold in tubs. Other types of crowdie are shaped into small logs and include *Gruth Dhu*, or Black Crowdie, which is blended with double cream then liberally coated in toasted rolled oats and black pepper. *Hramsa* is crowdie mixed with wild garlic and white and red pepper, while *Galic Hramsa* is rolled in crumbled hazelnuts and almonds.

**Caboc**, from the Highlands, is a soft-textured cream cheese shaped into logs and rolled in toasted pinhead oatmeal. The nubbly oatmeal contrasts well with the soft creamy cheese. The name is derived from the word *kebbock*, the old generic name for cheese.

**Dunsyre Blue** is an artisan-made, blue-veined, cow's-milk cheese with a creamy yet sharp flavour. It is made solely from the milk of native Ayrshire cattle, renowned for its excellence.

**Lanark Blue** is made from unpasteurized sheep's milk and is mottled with blue veins. Its creamy, sharp flavour is superb and the cheese has been compared favourably with the French Roquefort.

**Strathdon Blue** is a Highland cheese with a deliciously spicy flavour and delectable creamy smooth texture dotted with knobbly blue veins, which provide a pleasing contrast. It has won the Best Scottish Cheese at the British Cheese Awards twice in the last few years.

**Cairnsmore** is a prize-winning hard farmhouse cheese from Galloway. Aromatic and nutty, with the sweetness of caramel and burnt toffee, it ripens in seven to nine months.

**Scottish Cheddar** is mostly made from pasteurized cow's milk and is a hard cheese with a delicious nutty flavour. When young it has a mild taste, which becomes sharper and fuller flavoured as the cheese matures.

**Drumloch** is a full-fat hard pressed cheese similar to Cheddar, made from the milk of Guernsey cows in Scotland. It has a beautiful creamy texture, light golden colour and rich flavour.

**Isle of Mull** is a cream-coloured cow's-milk cheese, similar in flavour to Cheddar, but with an unmistakable tang of the sea.

**Tobermory** is an excellent full-flavoured, traditional unpasteurized farmhouse hard cheese, which is matured for 18 months.

**Tobermory Mornish** Made using sheep's milk, this is a silky smooth, semi-soft, white, mould-ripened cheese with a wonderful creamy flavour that has hints of grass and lemon.

**Orkney Farmhouse Cheese**, made with unpasteurized cow's milk, is renowned and has a wonderfully buttery, mellow flavour. Because of

Orkney's isolation, traditional small-scale cheese-making on farms there has continued for hundreds of years.

**Inverloch**, a superb hard-pressed, pasteurized goat's milk cheese coated in red wax, is made on the Isle of Gigha.

**Gigha Pear** and **Gigha Orange** These are innovative and attractive fruit-shaped waxed cheeses, which are a blend of Cheddar, cream cheese and flavourings such as pear liqueur and orange liqueur.

**St Andrews** from Perthshire is a creamy semi-soft cheese. It is one of the two Trappist-style washed-rind cheeses made in Scotland; the other is Bishop Kennedy. It has a supple, holey texture and a sweet-sour, slightly yeasty taste.

**Bishop Kennedy** has its origins in the medieval monasteries of France. A full-fat soft cheese, with a strong creamy taste, it is runny when ripe. The rind is washed in malt whisky to produce a distinctive orange-red crust. It has become popular in cooking.

***Below*** *Cairnsmore (top) is aromatic and nutty, while Caboc is creamy and rolled in toasted oatmeal.*

# From hedgerow and orchard

Flourishing for centuries in Scotland's long cool summers and fertile soil, fruits and berries play a key role in the Scottish kitchen. Wild strawberries (*Fragaria vesca*) and raspberries (*Rubus idaeus*) were once plentiful but are now scarce. The tiny berries have a magnificent flavour, different from that of today's cultivated berries.

In the past, wealthy people grew peaches in their gardens. In the 18th century, ovens built behind the garden walls supplemented the sun's heat and later in the same century, hollow walls with flues, heated by furnaces below the ground, provided a more efficient way of keeping in heat, allowing all kinds of delicate and exotic fruits to be grown. Cherries, apricots, blackcurrants, plums, gooseberries, strawberries, raspberries and blackberries were enjoyed as part of the summer diet and incorporated into recipes.

## Berries

The traditional Scottish kitchen garden would have berry bushes, especially raspberries, the national favourite. In

*Right Mulberries can be eaten just as they are when ripe.*

*Above Elderberries can be cooked in pies, tarts and fools or used to make jellies and sauces.*

Tayside, which is famous for its sweet velvety raspberries and juicy strawberries, there are pick-your-own fruit farms, where people rush to pick the berries in their prime, usually in July. If you pick your own fruit, go early in the morning or choose a cool day when the fruit will be in peak condition.

All types of berry are delicate and very perishable so keep them in the refrigerator and eat them as fresh as possible. Farm shops offer very good value, as the berries are usually freshly picked. Look for firm, plump berries,

*Left You will often find a bush of raspberries growing in a cottage garden or hedgerow.*

but remember that very large berries often lack flavour. To enjoy them at their best, allow them to reach room temperature before eating. Don't wash them until just before eating. Rinse strawberries very gently and hull them after washing to avoid making them soggy – the hull acts as a plug.

**Raspberries** from Scotland have acquired an excellent reputation and have been grown commercially since the beginning of the 20th century. Over the years new varieties have been developed, such as Glen Moy and Glen Garry.

**Blackberries** Glossy, juicy blackberries are one of late summer's most delicious fruits, and the most common wild fruit in Britain. Blackberries are known as brambles in Scotland and in the Highlands the bush is called *an druise beannaichte* – the blessed bramble.

**Tayberries** are a cross between the red raspberry and a strain of blackberry. They are very juicy with a sharp taste and make particularly good jam.

**Mulberries** are large berries, either black or white, that grow on large dome-shaped bushes, which can be very old. They make excellent jams, jellies and sauces.

**Loganberries** are large juicy dark red-wine coloured berries, a cross between raspberries and dewberries (which are in the same family as blackberries). They are used to flavour stews and drinks.

***Above*** *Cranachan, a delicious blend of juicy raspberries, thick, fresh cream and rolled oats, is a firm favourite as a dessert.*

**Strawberries** grow well in the Lowlands but have trouble ripening elsewhere. The delicious wild variety can be found in hedgerows, making wonderful treats.

**Elderberries** are a tasty addition to game and meat dishes. They grow on elder trees, following the blooming of the elderflower, and the berries can be used to flavour drinks and cordials.

**Gooseberries** are found in many kitchen gardens. The succulent bright green berries have a sharp flavour and make delicious pies and crumbles.

***Below*** *Victoria plums are large oval fruits with yellow skins flushed with scarlet and a lovely sweet juicy flesh. They are good for bottling and stewing.*

**Rowanberries** are tiny bright orange-red berries that are added to sauces and relishes for rich game meats.

**Rose hips** are the seed pods for roses, and appear after the plants have finished flowering. They make excellent jellies to serve with game.

### Orchard fruits

The Lowlands produce some wonderful and flavoursome orchard fruits, although the season is short. In addition to those below, peaches and cherries are also grown, if not widely.

**Apples** of many varieties are grown for eating and use in jams and jellies, as well as pies and crumbles.

**Pears** are also abundant, making fabulous preserves, jellies and pie fillings when they ripen in the autumn.

**Plums** grow well in the Lowlands and are a favourite in pies and crumbles, as well as with porridge (oatmeal). Victoria plums are the most commonly found.

### Jams and preserves

In the 18th century, when sugar became affordable to almost everyone, it became the vogue to make jams and preserves from seasonal fruits. Costly imported fruits, particularly oranges, were also used.

**Marmalades** Early marmalade had a strong flavour and was so dense and sticky that a knife was needed to slice it. Early Scottish recipes called the shreds of peel "chips" and

***Above*** *Scottish marmalades are known around the world for their excellent quality and flavour.*

so the product became known as chip marmalade. The Scots were the first to serve marmalade as a breakfast spread, as they believed that the peel and sugar warmed the stomach at the first meal of the day. They were also the first to produce a less thick and sticky marmalade, which became known as Scotch marmalade in England and was much in demand.

**Jams and jellies** have taken a prime place in the Scottish kitchen, especially those using the wealth of berries that grow wild in the countryside and are cultivated in the garden.

They were primarily made to stock the larder with fruits and berries to last the winter, by the 18th century jam-making had become more of an art-form and cooks in big estates took pride in the quality of their recipes.

Recently jam- and jelly-making has had a new lease of life. The growth in cottage industries and a growing demand for traditional, organic and non-manufactured goods have given rise to a number of small preserve-makers. They produce some excellent and delicious jams and jellies.

# Wild mushrooms

Throughout Scotland's long history, wild mushrooms have been used to flavour many dishes, especially soups, stews and casseroles. They thrive in damp woods and grassy meadows, making the Scottish climate and landscape ideal for growth.

Although there are plenty of cultivated varieties available today, the flavour of wild mushrooms is far superior, with each variety having its own texture and taste.

In Scotland wild mushrooms, both fresh and dried, are becoming more easily available from specialist stores, grocers and local markets.

**Button (white) mushrooms** have an excellent flavour, and they sprout abundantly during the warm months, especially after rain. Commonly found, these mushrooms impart a definite, faintly sweet taste when added to soups and stews. Larger varieties are called closed-cap mushrooms.

**Common field (portabello) mushrooms** are pink and white when young and turn brown then almost black as they age. Small and unopened the mushrooms have a delicate flavour, while the taste of older specimens is more pronounced.

*Below Field blewits add a nutty flavour to soups and stews.*

*Above Clockwise from top: flat or field mushrooms, chestnut mushrooms, button mushrooms, and closed-cap mushrooms.*

**Chanterelle mushrooms** are a beautiful golden yellow with a fleshy cap, curly edge and the fragrance of apricots. They flourish in large groups in summer and autumn in woods, especially those of beech and oak. Chanterelles have a special affinity with potatoes and eggs, and are delicious in cream sauces.

**Field blewits** or blue leg mushrooms are found in long grass or pastureland. They have a buff-coloured cap and the flesh is quite thick and chunky, good to use in soups and stews.

**Morel mushrooms** rate among the finest wild mushrooms and, unlike most other edible mushrooms, appear in orchards and forests in the spring. Morels have a honeycombed appearance and a splendid meaty, slightly nutty flavour that is enhanced by cooking in butter. Morels come in various colours – reddish, grey, black or brown – and their intense aromatic flavour is not lost when they are dried. Morels are never eaten raw, as they are likely to cause stomach upsets.

**Cep mushrooms** are also known as penny buns. These are highly prized with a wonderfully nutty flavour. Found in woodland, they can grow to be very big – up to 1kg (2lb 2oz). Check for maggots before eating.

**St George's mushrooms** are found in pastures. They have a delicious nutty flavour and meaty aroma, and can be fried, stewed or boiled.

**Puffballs** range in diameter from less than 2.5cm/1in to more than 30cm/12in and are among the best of the edible mushrooms. When young and firm they are delicious sliced and fried or grilled (broiled). As they mature, the interior turns yellow, which is a sign that they are no longer worth eating. The pear-shaped puffball grows on rotting logs and stumps, in late summer and early autumn. You should take great care when collecting puffball mushrooms from the wild as they can closely resemble more poisonous varieties.

*Left* Tasty chanterelles are delicious in cream sauces.

### Mushroom picking

Never be tempted to pick wild mushrooms unless you are an expert or are accompanied by a mycologist. Some deadly poisonous mushrooms look remarkably similar to edible varieties. If you add just one poisonous mushroom to a basket of edible varieties, your whole harvest will be tainted and must be disposed of.

There are many books that will help you to identify wild fungi but the best way of finding out more is by going on one of the many organized mushroom forays that are available for novice wild-mushroom enthusiasts. In Scotland there is the Scottish Wild Mushroom Code, but wherever you are picking you should act sensibly. Wildlife needs mushrooms too, so only pick what you will use. Do not pick mushrooms until the cap has opened out, and leave those that are past their best. The main part of the mushroom is below the surface; take care not to damage or trample it and not to disturb its surroundings. Sprinkle trimmings discretely in the same area as the mushroom came from.

Some mushrooms are also rare and should not be picked. Before you collect mushrooms at a nature reserve please always seek advice from the manager. Special conditions may apply to some areas where rare species are being encouraged.

*Below* Chanterelle mushrooms can be found in damp woodland in late summer and autumn.

*Above* Ceps, also known as penny buns, have a lovely nutty flavour.

### Dried mushrooms

Many types of wild mushroom can be bought dried and can add excellent flavour. It takes 900g/2lb of fresh mushrooms to obtain just 90g/3½oz dried mushrooms. The flavour of dried mushrooms is concentrated and their rich, strong flavour means a little goes a long way – just 25g/1oz of dried mushrooms mixed with 450g/1lb of fresh mushrooms will flavour an entire dish. Dried wild mushrooms can be added to risottos, soups, sauces and stews, or they may be fried in butter. To reconstitute them, soak in hot water for 20–30 minutes before cooking. Use a half-water, half-milk mixture for morel mushrooms. Always add the soaking liquid to the dish, as much of the flavour remains in the liquid, but strain it first to remove any grit or dirt.

# Vegetables from the kitchen garden

Medieval French monks brought many hitherto unknown varieties of fruits and vegetables, such as spinach, French (green) beans and cauliflower, to Scotland. The monks of Holyrood planted orchards and laid out gardens at the base of the Castle Rock in Edinburgh, and trained laymen in horticulture. The cultivation of vegetables and fruits spread to the gardens of the nobility and other wealthy families and by the 19th century Scottish gardeners had become internationally famous.

## Green vegetables

Young summer vegetables were used to make *hairst bree*, harvest broth, which is similar to Scotch broth but without the barley. The tender sweet vegetables gave the broth a special flavour.
**Kale or kail** Dark green leafy kale is eaten throughout Scotland and is so central to Scottish cuisine that the word *kail* came to mean soup and even to signify the main meal of the day. Kale grows on a long stem and has

curly dark green leaves but no head. It has the advantage of flourishing in Scotland's often harsh climate and is resistant to frost – in fact the flavour improves after a slight frost. Shred the leaves finely and cook for a few minutes in boiling salted water, as for cabbage. In Shetland a unique variety of kale develops a head. It is believed to have ancient Scandinavian origins.
**Cabbage** was a staple item of the diet in Orkney and Shetland (in common with Scandinavian countries) and was eaten as a vegetable in its own right and included in soups and stews. Cabbage was preserved for winter by being layered in barrels with fat, oats, salt and spices with a weight on top. It was then left to ferment, the result being very similar to sauerkraut.
**Leeks** have a delicate onion flavour. The market gardeners on the Lothian coast supplied fruit and vegetables to Edinburgh and the quality of their leeks was unsurpassed. Scottish leeks are distinct from other leeks as they have almost as much green as white, so add a good colour to broths. They are essential to the famous cock-a-leekie

***Above*** *Leeks are a crucial ingredient for traditional cock-a-leekie and potato and leek soups, as well as many stews.*

soup, a broth made with chicken and leeks. Slice leeks down the middle and wash very well to remove any sand or grit. Chop and add to soups or stews.

## Wild leaves

**Nettles** Highlanders once gathered young tender nettles in the spring to eat alone as a vegetable or in soups and broths. Young nettle leaves can be cooked in the same way as spinach. Wash them well and place in a pan with just the water clinging to the leaves. Cook over a low heat for 7–10 minutes, chopping them as they cook in the pan, then add butter, salt and pepper to taste.
**Wild rocket** grows prolifically in many areas, especially in the

***Left*** *From far left: white cabbage, savoy cabbage and green cabbage are usually boiled or steamed.*

**Above** *Mashed turnips make up the traditional dish of "bashed neeps", also known as "turnip purry".*

Lowlands alongside gardens and pastures. It can be picked, washed and added to stews or made into a fresh peppery salad.

**Wild garlic leaves** are found in meadows and alongside pastures. They are only around for a few weeks in the year. They add a delicate, mild garlic flavour to dishes.

### Root vegetables

**Carrots** In the days when sugar was a costly imported luxury, most people relied on honey to sweeten their food, together with the natural sweetness of root vegetables, particularly carrots. Their inherent natural sweetness and moist texture made them a successful ingredient of many delicious cakes, puddings, pies, tarts and preserves.

**Turnips** were introduced into Scotland in the 18th century and the Scots recognized them immediately as a tasty vegetable – unlike the English who fed them to their cattle. Several Scottish dishes use turnips and they became the traditional accompaniment to haggis.

**Right** *Potatoes, known in Scotland as "tatties", are commonly mashed.*

Mashed turnips were commonly known as *bashed neeps*, or *turnip purry* (from the French purée) by the gentry. Young turnips have the best flavour and texture.

**Potatoes** were an important crop in the west and in the Islands and by the 19th century had become a staple food. Potatoes form the basis of many old dishes and in general Scots prefer floury varieties such as Maris Piper, Golden Wonder and Kerr's Pinks. *Mealy tatties* (boiled potatoes) were cheap and filling, and were sold from carts in Scottish cites in the 19th century. *Stovies* is a very old dish consisting of sliced potatoes cooked with onions. Sometimes cheese or meat was added to make the dish more substantial. In Orkney cooked potatoes and turnips or kale were mashed together to make *clapshot*. The

**Above** *Parsnips are a great favourite, either mashed or roasted.*

curiously named *rumbledethumps*, from the Border region, is made with potatoes and cabbage. The name comes from "rumbled and thumped". *Colcannon* is a Highland dish of boiled cabbage, carrots, turnips and potatoes mashed with butter.

# Oats and barley

Scotland's cool climate is ideal for oats and barley. Rolled oats are used in oatcakes, bread, broth and of course porridge (oatmeal). Oatcakes have a light, mealy flavour and may be thick or thin – it is a matter of personal preference. Highly nutritious, they were eaten by 14th-century soldiers to sustain them during long marches. In the past, oatcakes accompanied almost every meal and they are delicious eaten with butter, cheese or marmalade.

## Oats and oatmeal

Used in a variety of foods and dishes, oats were also used to make black and white mealie puddings. Mealie pudding is a mixture of oats, onions, suet (chilled, grated shortening) and seasoning boiled in a skin or cloth; blood was added to make black pudding (blood sausage). These puddings were traditionally made in the winter when the animals were slaughtered. Skirlie was made by mixing oats, onions and suet, and frying the mixture in a pan. The noise, or skirl, as it cooked gave rise to the name. Today it is usually served with roast meat or used as a stuffing.

Soups and broths have an important role and a long history in Scotland's cuisine. *Brose* is an ancient dish and a distant relative of the modern Swiss muesli (granola). It was quick to

*Above Porridge (oatmeal) has now been recognized as a delicious and healthy way to start the day.*

make, nourishing and filling. A labourer or shepherd would fill a leather or wooden hoggin (wallet or pouch) with ground oats, then add water from a nearby stream or brook. The hoggin was slung on his back and the continuous warmth and movement as he worked caused the mixture to thicken and ferment. A simple meal could also be made by mixing oats with boiling water – perhaps the world's first convenience food. The term *brose* has gradually come to mean a variety of different broths thickened with rolled oats, such as *mussel brose* and *kail brose*.

Porridge came to be accepted throughout the British Empire as a breakfast dish. In the 18th century it

*Above*
*Clockwise from top: rolled oats, oatmeal, whole oats and oat bran.*

*Right* Clockwise from left:
*pot barley, barley flakes
and pearl barley.*

was usual to add ale or
porter to the porridge, and
on bitterly cold winter
mornings a couple of spoonfuls
of whisky were added – even for
children to sustain them on their
long walk to school. A bowl of milk
or cream was placed next to the
porridge bowl and a spoon was dipped
first into the hot porridge then into the
cold milk or cream. In Scotland it is still
customary to add salt – never sugar –
to porridge, with cold milk or thin
cream as an accompaniment.

Leftover porridge was poured into the
porridge drawer of the dresser and left
to set, after which it was cut into slices,
known as *caulders*. They were taken by
farm workers to the fields and eaten in
the middle of the day. Sometimes the
slices were cooked alongside eggs,
bacon or fish.

Quaker Oats created rolled oats in
the United States in 1877. Made by
steaming and rolling the oats, rolled
oats have the advantage of cooking
quickly, but there is some loss of flavour
and nutrients due to the heat
treatment. Rolled oats are particularly
popular in Scotland.

### Barley

Bread made with barley was widely
eaten throughout Scotland until the
end of the 17th century, when oats
became the more popular grain, one
reason being that they keep longer than
barley. However, in the Highlands and
Islands barley continued as a staple.

Barley is still a common thickener for
broths, soups and sauces; it is a crucial
ingredient of the famous Scotch broth,
Scotland's favourite soup. Much of the
crop today is malted and used in the
making of whisky.

Bere, an ancient variety of
barley, has been grown and ground for
food since the Stone Age. Centuries
ago this type of barley was called *bygg*,
which is the name given to barley in
Norway. In Orkney the crop was called
corn and provided the staple food in
the form of bere bannocks and home-
brewed ale. Bere was used by the
whisky and beer industry until the 20th
century, but its higher protein and

lower starch content
is no longer favoured.
Farmers also prefer
modern types of barley,
as the yield is greater than
that of bere.

Bere is still cultivated in
Orkney where it is kiln-dried
and stone-ground to produce
beremeal. Creamy coloured
beremeal has a more earthy
flavour than that of commercially
produced barley flour. It is used
to make bread and bannocks by
bakers in Orkney and the Hebrides,
although a small amount of wheat
flour is now usually added to lighten
the texture.

Buy rolled oats and barley flour in
small quantities from a store with a
high turnover, so you know they will be
fresh. Store in an airtight container.

*Below* Oatcakes are delicious spread
*with butter and marmalade or
served with a variety of cheeses.*

# Bannocks and bread

Bannocks cooked from the bakestone and the variety of savoury and sweet breads have always been a part of the Scottish diet. Recently there has been an upsurge of interest in "real" bannocks and bread, and traditional, well-flavoured bannocks and crusty breads from dedicated bakers, who are masters of their craft, are once again in demand. Their recipes go back to the first bannocks.

## Bannocks

The traditional bannocks are thicker and softer than oatcakes, although similar in make-up. Their name probably comes from the Latin word for bread, *panis*. Bannocks are unique to Scotland and were originally unleavened in the days when peat was the only fuel available and every home had a

*Below Bannocks are cooked on a heated bakestone in thin rounds traditionally cut into wedges.*

bakestone on which the bannocks were freshly cooked or fired each day. They became less popular when domestic ovens became more widespread, but have regained a market with the recent resurgence of traditional foods and recipes.

## The first breads

The advent of ovens in the 16th century led to baked loaves, and every town possessed a public bakehouse where bread dough was taken to be baked. In the more populous towns and cities those who could afford it bought their bread from the baker's store. The Baijen Hole was an ancient and famous baker's store in Edinburgh. It was renowned for its rolls, called *soutar's clods*, which had a thick crust and were made from coarse wheat flour.

In 16th-century Scotland there were four kinds of wheat bread. The best was *manche*, followed by *cheat* (trencher bread, used as a plate),

*Above Rowies are buttery bread rolls traditionally eaten for breakfast with homemade jams and jellies.*

*ravelled* and *mashlock*. Wheat was grown in the fertile Lowlands, but bread made from wheat flour was eaten only by the wealthy, right up until the early part of the 20th century, when it gradually became a staple food for everyone. Regional speciality breads developed throughout Scotland.

**Rowies** Aberdeen buttery rowies or butteries are very similar to French croissants, but taste saltier and are flatter in shape. They are associated with Aberdeen because the fishing fleets used to take them on their journeys into cold, rough seas. The high fat content of the rowies kept out the bitter cold and sustained the men. The rolls are quite difficult to make at home as professional bakers steam the dough before baking.

**Baps** (the origin of the name is unknown) are floury rolls, which today are mostly round in shape, although originally the shape and size varied from one region to another. Baps are thickly coated with flour before baking to prevent a crust forming, which allows them to rise well. Prime Minister William Gladstone's grandfather owned a small store in Edinburgh that sold baps, along with flour and oats. His

*Left Scottish morning rolls, or baps, are soft and slightly flattened.*

baps were rumoured to be small, and so the neighbourhood lads nicknamed him "Sma' Baps".

**Fadge** is a large flat loaf or cake, sometimes with dried fruit and nuts.

**Tod**, or toddie, is a small round cake of bread that was given to children.

**Whig** (meaning wedge) is a fine wheat teabread that can be buttered.

**Ankerstoek** is a large loaf of rye bread.

**Buttermilk bread** is quick and easy to make and can be made with oats or wheat flour.

### Breads for special occasions

The breads and cakes that were specially prepared for festive occasions were collectively known as *gudebread*. Selkirk bannock is a round yeasted fruit loaf, first baked in 1859 by Robbie Douglas in his bakery at Selkirk Market Place. He introduced several features that improved the local bannock. Indeed, when Queen Victoria visited Sir Walter Scott's granddaughter in 1867, she declined the splendid repast that had been prepared for her in favour of a piece of Selkirk bannock and a cup of tea.

*Right Bread made from wheat flour was only eaten by the wealthy in the Lowlands until the mid-19th century.*

### Milling and bread manufacture

In the mid-19th century, white flour became cheaper than brown and the introduction of roller-milling, which left only the white part of the wheat, but removed the germ and husk, meant that everyone could now afford white bread. It was sold cheaply in every corner store and a slice of bread and butter became a basic part of working-class meals.

A cutting loaf was slightly cheaper than a fresh loaf and was usually a day old when sold, as it sliced more easily than freshly baked bread.

Plain loaves were baked in batches and joined together without the use of baking tins (pans), then separated once they were cooked. A pan loaf, baked in a tin, was for the wealthier people. "Speaking pan loafy" meant speaking in an affected manner, while "a pan loaf" was a slang expression for somebody who acted posh.

In the 1950s and early 60s many of the country's small traditional bakers were ousted by the large milling companies, but there is a strong recent trend towards the tasty traditional breads of the past and many small producers are proving successful.

# A wealth of cakes

The humble bannock, cooked on a bakestone over a peat fire, had, by the 15th century, developed into a Scottish speciality, the rich fruity teabread. This was made by adding expensive dried fruits, honey, butter and spices to plain bread dough. At this time, dried fruits and sugar, which was regarded as a spice, were kept under lock and key along with other expensive spices such as ginger and pepper. These breads were served only on special occasions.

### The Scottish fruitcake

In the bakehouses and kitchens of the wealthy, teabreads gave way to enormous fruitcakes baked in large ovens, which were served on important occasions. There are a great many Scottish recipes for fruitcakes.

**Dundee cake** No one can agree what goes to make an authentic Dundee cake and where it originated. It has been suggested that it is a descendant of Dundee gingerbread, or that the

recipe was devised by the marmalade makers as a means of using up the surplus orange peel. Others believe that marmalade was one of the original ingredients of the cake. Dundee cake should be lighter and more crumbly than traditional fruit

*Left The traditional round fruitcake, upon which many regional specialities were based.*

cake, not too heavily fruited, and should have the characteristic topping of whole or split almonds, without which it's not a genuine Dundee cake.

**Plum cake** These early cakes were shaped by hand into rounds and wrapped in pastry (known as *huff* pastry). This was then placed inside a tin hoop placed on a tin tray before baking. The pastry protected the outside of the cake from burning during the long cooking needed for such a large cake, and also, together with the tin hoop, helped to keep the cake in shape. The *huff* pastry was carefully cut off and discarded before the cake was served.

**Black bun** The traditional Hogmanay cake is a rich, dark fruit cake encased in pastry. Bun is the old Scots word for plum cake, as the cakes were originally made wth dried plums. The pastry protected the outside of the cake from burning during cooking and helped to keep the cake in shape. The fruit-

*Left Dundee cake, with its topping of almonds, has become a favourite traditional fruit cake throughout Britain.*

***Above*** *The rich, pastry-covered black bun is celebrated with a few whiskies at Hogmanay.*

***Above*** *Sponge cakes came to Scotland in the 19th century, with a range of flavours and toppings.*

***Above*** *Glamis cake with walnuts and dates became a popular cake to eat as part of high tea.*

soaked pastry was discarded. Today the pastry is richer and is an essential part of the cake.

## Sponge cakes

The early 19th century saw the introduction of coal-fired ranges with ovens and this, together with a dramatic fall in the prices of wheat and sugar, meant that Scottish women could bake at home. Plain cakes without fruit became popular and were intended to be eaten with a cup of the newly popular tea. Plain cakes were also far cheaper and less time-consuming to make than fruitcakes, and could be flavoured or decorated.

By the 19th century it was discovered that adding fat to the sponge mixture made a more substantial cake with better keeping qualities. High tea became an important meal, especially in the industrial towns. A tempting array of sponge cakes, pastries and fancies would always be on offer when visitors were expected.

## Regional cakes

Every region of Scotland developed its own unique and delicious recipes for cakes and teabreads. Some of

Scotland's regional cake recipes went on to become world famous, while others virtually disappeared from baker's stores and tearooms. A large variety of regional cakes are still baked today.

**Deer horns** are fried cakes formed around cornet-shaped tins.

**Coburg cakes** are popular for their spicy taste.

**Glamis cake** is made with walnuts and dates, squeezed together in a loaf tin and cut into rich slices.

**Montrose cakes** are flavoured with rose water and nutmeg.

***Below*** *Honeys produced in the Lowlands add sweetness to many traditional cakes.*

**Scots snow cake** uses arrowroot instead of flour.

**Sair heidies**, from the Grampian region, are small sponge cakes wrapped in paper jackets and covered with crushed sugar crystals.

**Balmoral cake** is unusual because of its baked almond-paste icing.

**Auld reekie plum cake** is a popular cake, containing whisky and ginger as well as dried fruits.

**Portree plum cake** from the Isle of Skye contains stout and spices.

**Kirrie loaf**, a teabread from Angus, is made with sultanas (golden raisins) and strong tea in the ingredients.

**Angus fruit cake** is made with honey and apples.

**Caraway seed cake** is a Scottish favourite, and almost always featured at funerals.

# Scotch whisky

Scotland's gift to the world, Scotch whisky is unique and inimitable. It requires the Scottish climate, pure water and rich peat, not to mention hundreds of years of experience in the skilful art of distilling.

The origins of whisky are lost in the mists of time. The word itself is derived from the Gaelic *uisge beatha* – the water of life. As time passed, *uisge* became *usky*, then eventually whisky. The oldest reference to whisky dates back to 1494 when "8 bolls of malt to Friar John Cor wherewith to make aquavitae" were entered in the Scottish Exchequer Rolls.

Scotland's national drink was already well established by the 15th century and by the early 1500s had also become the favoured drink of royalty. During the 17th century the popularity

of whisky grew steadily, especially in the Lowlands where many distilleries sprang up to meet the increasing demand. Highland distilleries were smaller than those of the south and supplied mainly local towns and villages.

In 1690 came the first mention of a famous whisky noted for its quality: Ferintosh, which was distilled by Forbes of Culloden. In 1784 the owner was bought out and Robert Burns immortalized the sad event:

*Thee Ferintosh! O sadly lost!*
*Scotland laments frae coast to coast!*

Cheap whisky became available in the 18th century, although it was rather nasty by all accounts, but good whisky, from Glenlivet for instance, was highly esteemed and expensive.

Whisky, especially malt whisky, is a versatile ingredient and its special taste imparts a distinctive yet subtle flavour to all kinds of dishes. Many of today's leading Scottish chefs have created marvellous recipes using whisky. Add a splash to a steaming bowl of those great stalwarts of Scottish cuisine, cock-a-leekie soup and Scotch broth.

Stir a couple of spoonfuls into a marinade for meat, game or poultry. Soak dried fruits for a rich fruitcake in whisky, then feed the baked cake with whisky. Not only does whisky add a unique flavour, it also preserves and tenderizes; for instance fish and meat can be marinated in whisky before cooking. Do not be afraid to experiment by using

***Above*** *The barley is initially malted, which means that it is soaked in tanks of spring water, known as steeps, for two to three days.*

different whiskies in a recipe; you will find that the taste of the whole dish is transformed.

## Malt whisky

Aromatic, smooth and full of complex character, malt whisky is a drink of enormous variety and no two malts are the same. Single malts are the products of just one distillery and are the most highly prized. Vatted malts are a blend of malts from several distilleries within a particular region. Malt whiskies, with their complex flavours, vary in colour from palest straw to deep glowing amber and are more expensive than blended whiskies. This is partly due to their long maturation in casks that have previously contained sherry, port, rum or bourbon – which also augment their flavour and character as well as colour; for instance a fino sherry cask produces a light-coloured whisky, while an oloroso sherry cask results in a darker, strongly sherried whisky. Each region

***Left*** *Laphroaig, made on Islay, is very peaty, and Whyte & Mackay is re-blended for a second period of maturation.*

*Left The Famous Grouse and Glenmorangie are both made in the northern Highlands.*

Lochnagar, produced close to Balmoral, is a typical example of a good East Highland malt.
**The Lowlands** produce malts which were the first whiskies to be drunk on a large scale, such as Rosebank. They have a fruity sweetness and a dry finish.
**Campbeltown** malts, from the Kintyre peninsula, are fully flavoured with a tang of salt, for example Springbank.
**Islay** produces dry, peaty and smoky malts. Some, such as Lavagulin, are powerful, while others, for example Bunnahabhain, are less so.

### Blended whiskies

Blending malt and grain whiskies has created some excellent whiskies. Master blenders may combine more than 50 different malt and grain whiskies into a blended whisky. The normal ratio of grain to malt is 60:40. The percentage of malt used

*Above Quality Scotch whisky should be enjoyed on its own or with ice.*

determines the quality, flavour, smoothness and character. Each whisky used in the blending process will usually have been matured for about five years, but there are also several longer-aged blended Scotch whiskies available.

*Below The casks are specially made from woods such as oak to impart a subtle flavour to the whisky.*

produces its own character, often expressing age-old traditions.
**Speyside** is the principal whisky-producing region and makes some of the world's greatest malts – Macallan, Glenfiddich and Glenlivet to name just three. Speyside malt whiskies are sweet and can be highly perfumed, with scents of roses, apples and lemonade.
**The Central Highlands** produce malt whiskies that are not so sweet. They tend to have a dry finish and a fine fragrance. Edradour is one example.
**West Highland** malts have a mild smokiness and a dryish finish, and include such fine whiskies as Talisker from the Isle of Skye.
**East Highland** malts are smooth and slightly sweet, with a hint of smokiness and a dryish finish. Royal

# Soups and appetizers

There has long been a tradition of soup making in Scotland. In rural areas it was usual for everyone to grow sufficient vegetables for the household in a kitchen garden, and these, plus a small amount of meat or a bone, would be added to a rich stock to make a healthy supper to feed the whole family. The sensational smoked salmons that are now being produced provide a sumptuous start to any meal, simply sprinkled with ground black pepper and a squeeze of fresh lemon. Other smoked products, game and wonderful cheeses also make delicious first courses.

# Spiced creamed parsnip soup with sherry

Parsnips are a naturally sweet vegetable and the modern addition of curry powder complements this perfectly, while a dash of sherry lifts the soup into the dinner-party realm. Try swirling some natural yogurt into this deeply flavoured dish when serving.

**2** Cut the parsnips into even-sized pieces, add to the pan and coat with butter. Stir in the curry powder.

**3** Pour in the sherry and cover with a cartouche (see Cook's Tip) and a lid. Cook over a low heat for 10 minutes or until the parsnips are softened, making sure they do not colour.

**4** Add the stock and season to taste. Bring to the boil then simmer for about 15 minutes or until the parsnips are soft. Remove from the heat. Allow to cool for a while then purée in a blender.

**5** When ready to serve, reheat the soup and check the seasoning. Add a swirl of natural (plain) yogurt, if you like.

**Serves 4**

115g/4oz/½ cup butter

2 onions, sliced

1kg /2¼lb parsnips, peeled

10ml/2 tsp curry powder

30ml/2 tbsp medium sherry

1.2 litres/2 pints/5 cups chicken or vegetable stock

salt and ground black pepper

**1** Melt the butter in a pan, add the onions and sweat gently without allowing them to colour.

**Cook's Tip**
A cartouche is a circle of greaseproof (waxed) paper that helps to keep in the moisture, so the vegetables cook in their own juices along with the sherry.

**Per portion** Energy 437kcal/1820kJ; Protein 5.9g; Carbohydrate 39.5g, of which sugars 20.2g; Fat 28.7g, of which saturates 16.8g; Cholesterol 67mg; Calcium 134mg; Fibre 12.9g; Sodium 218mg.

# Leek and potato soup

This is a hearty Scottish staple, forming everything from a warming lunch to a hot drink from a flask by the loch on a cold afternoon. The chopped vegetables produce a chunky soup. If you prefer a smooth texture, press the mixture through a sieve.

**Serves 4**

50g/2oz/¼ cup butter

2 leeks, washed and chopped

1 small onion, peeled and finely chopped

350g/12oz potatoes, peeled and chopped

900ml/1½ pints/3¾ cups chicken or vegetable stock

salt and ground black pepper

chopped fresh parsley, to garnish

**2** Add the potatoes to the pan and cook for about 2–3 minutes, then add the stock and bring to the boil. Cover and simmer for 30–35 minutes.

**3** Season to taste and remove the pan from the heat. Dice and stir in the remaining butter. Garnish with the chopped parsley and serve hot.

**1** Heat 25g/1oz/2 tbsp of the butter in a large pan over a medium heat. Add the leeks and onion and cook gently, stirring occasionally, for about 7 minutes, until they are softened but not browned.

**Cook's Tips**
• Don't use a food processor to purée this soup as it can give the potatoes a gluey consistency. The potatoes should be left to crumble and disintegrate naturally as they boil, making the consistency of the soup thicker the longer you leave them.
• If you can, make your own chicken or vegetable stock by simmering bones and vegetables in water for 2 hours and straining the liquid.

**Per portion** Energy 179Kcal/747kJ; Protein 3.2g; Carbohydrate 17.9g, of which sugars 4g; Fat 11g, of which saturates 6.7g; Cholesterol 27mg; Calcium 32mg; Fibre 3g; Sodium 88mg.

# Rocket soup with kiln-smoked salmon

Kiln-smoked salmon has actually been "cooked" during the smoking process, producing a delicious flaky texture. This is in contrast to traditional cold-smoked salmon, which is not actually cooked but does not spoil because it has been preserved first in brine.

**Serves 4**

15ml/1 tbsp olive oil

1 small onion, sliced

1 garlic clove, crushed

150ml/¼ pint/⅔ cup double (heavy) cream

350ml/12fl oz/1½ cups vegetable stock

350g/12oz rocket (arugula)

4 fresh basil leaves

salt and ground black pepper

flaked kiln-smoked salmon, to garnish

**1** Put the olive oil in a high-sided pan over a medium heat and allow to heat up. Add the sliced onion and sweat for a few minutes, stirring continuously. Add the garlic and continue to sweat gently until soft and transparent, although you should not allow the onion to colour.

**2** Add the cream and stock, stir in gently and bring slowly to the boil. Allow to simmer gently for about 5 minutes. Add the rocket, reserving a few leaves to garnish, and the basil. Return briefly to the boil and turn off the heat. Add a little cold water and allow to cool for a few minutes.

**3** Purée in a blender until smooth, adding a little salt and pepper to taste. When ready to serve, reheat gently but do not allow to boil. Serve in warmed bowls with a few flakes of salmon, a leaf or two of rocket and a drizzle of virgin olive oil over the top.

**Variation**
Cold-smoked salmon is also very good with this soup, and can be used if you can't find the kiln-smoked variety. Simply cut a few slices into medium to thick strips and add to the hot soup. Warming the smoked salmon for a few minutes increases the flavour.

**Per portion** Energy 258kcal/1063kJ; Protein 6.8g; Carbohydrate 3.2g, of which sugars 2.8g; Fat 24.3g, of which saturates 13.1g; Cholesterol 56mg; Calcium 174mg; Fibre 2.1g; Sodium 395mg.

# Cullen skink

The famous Cullen skink comes from the small fishing port of Cullen on the east coast of Scotland, the word "skink" meaning an essence or soup. The fishermen smoked their smaller fish and these, with locally grown potatoes, formed their staple diet.

**Serves 6**

1 Finnan haddock, about 350g/12oz

1 onion, chopped

bouquet garni

900ml/1½ pints/3¾ cups water

500g/1¼lb potatoes, quartered

600ml/1 pint/2½ cups milk

40g/1½oz/3 tbsp butter

salt and pepper

chopped chives, to garnish

**1** Put the haddock, onion, bouquet garni and water into a large pan and bring to the boil. Skim the surface with a slotted spoon, discarding any fish skin, then cover the pan. Reduce the heat and gently poach for 10–15 minutes, until the fish flakes easily.

**2** Lift the fish from the pan, using a fish slice, and remove the skin and any bones. Return the skin and bones to the pan and simmer, uncovered, for a further 30 minutes. Flake the cooked fish flesh and leave to cool.

**Cook's Tip**
If you can't find Finnan haddock, use a good quality smoked haddock.

**3** Strain the fish stock and return to the pan, then add the potatoes and simmer for about 25 minutes, or until tender.

**4** Carefully remove the poatoes from the pan using a slotted spoon. Add the milk to the pan and bring to the boil.

**5** In a separate pan, mash the potatoes with the butter. A little at a time, whisk this thoroughly into the pan until the soup is thick and creamy.

**6** Add the flaked fish to the pan and adjust the seasoning. Sprinkle with chives and serve immediately with fresh crusty bread.

**Per portion** Energy 205kcal/864kJ; Protein 16.1g; Carbohydrate 19g, of which sugars 6.4g; Fat 7.8g, of which saturates 4.7g; Cholesterol 41mg; Calcium 137mg; Fibre 1g; Sodium 132mg.

# Shore crab soup

These little crabs have a velvet feel to their shell. They are mostly caught off the west coast of Scotland, although they can be quite difficult to find in fishmongers. If you have trouble finding them, you can also use common or brown crabs for this recipe.

**Serves 4**

1kg/2¼lbs shore or velvet crabs

50g/2oz/¼ cup butter

50g/2oz leek, washed and chopped

50g/2oz carrot, chopped

30ml/2 tbsp brandy

225g/8oz ripe tomatoes, chopped

15ml/1 tbsp tomato purée (paste)

120ml/4fl oz/½ cup dry white wine

1.5 litres/2½ pints/6¼ cups fish stock

sprig of fresh tarragon

60ml/4 tbsp double (heavy) cream

lemon juice

**1** Bring a large pan of water to a rolling boil and plunge the live crabs into it. They will be killed very quickly, and the bigger the pan and the more water there is, the better. Once the crabs are dead – a couple of minutes at most – take them out of the water, place in a large bowl and smash them up. This can be done with either a wooden mallet or the end of a rolling pin.

**2** Melt the butter in a heavy pan, add the leek and carrot and cook gently until soft but not coloured.

**3** Add the crabs and when very hot pour in the brandy, stirring to allow the flavour to pervade the whole pan. Add the tomatoes, tomato purée, wine, stock and tarragon. Bring to the boil and simmer gently for 30 minutes.

**4** Strain the soup through a metal sieve, forcing as much of the tomato mixture through as possible. (If you like you could remove the big claws and purée the remains in a blender.)

**5** Return to the heat, simmer for a few minutes then season to taste. Add the cream and lemon juice, and serve.

**Cook's Tip**
If you don't have fish stock then water will do, or you could use some of the water used to boil the crabs initially.

Per portion Energy 419kcal/1741kJ; Protein 35.1g; Carbohydrate 3.8g, of which sugars 3.6g; Fat 25.7g, of which saturates 15.1g; Cholesterol 196mg; Calcium 252mg; Fibre 1.1g; Sodium 1122mg.

# King scallops in Jerusalem artichoke broth

In Scotland scallops are mainly found on the west coast and around the Islands. The best are hand-collected, when divers literally dive down and collect them from the seabed. This way, the divers can be selective and choose only the right size, and they do not disturb the seabed.

**Serves 4**

450g/1lb Jerusalem artichokes

75g/3oz/6 tbsp butter

1 large onion, chopped

5ml/1 tsp sea salt

120ml/4 fl oz/½ cup double (heavy) cream

8 fresh king scallops

chopped fresh parsley, to garnish

**1** Roughly peel the artichokes, but don't be too fussy as the knobbly bits can be hard to get into and it is very time-consuming. It is most important to remove all the earth otherwise the soup can be gritty. Chop roughly.

**2** Heat a pan, melt the butter and gently sweat the onions until softened but not coloured.

**3** Add the artichokes and stir to coat in the butter.

**4** Cover the pan with a well-fitting lid and leave to stew gently for about 10 minutes, giving the pan a shake occasionally to prevent the artichokes from sticking to the base of the pan.

**5** Pour in enough water just to cover the artichokes, and add the salt. Bring to the boil then reduce the heat and simmer gently for 30 minutes. Purée in a blender until smooth, then strain into a clean pan. Add the cream and check the seasoning.

**6** Slice the scallops in two horizontally. When the soup is ready, remove from the heat and add the scallops. They will cook in the soup off the heat in a couple of minutes. Serve garnished with chopped fresh parsley, allowing four slices of scallop per person.

**Per portion** Energy 383kcal/1586kJ; Protein 13.5g; Carbohydrate 8.1g, of which sugars 5g; Fat 33.3g, of which saturates 20.4g; Cholesterol 106mg; Calcium 94mg; Fibre 2.1g; Sodium 280mg.

# Asparagus with lime butter dip

In Scotland asparagus has the shortest of seasons, just six weeks, but it is worth the wait and while it is at its freshest you should find as many ways as possible to enjoy it. This recipe is based on the traditional butter sauce but it has lime added to lift the flavour. The dip can be used for most kinds of shellfish too.

**Serves 4**

40 medium asparagus spears

1 litre/1¾ pints/4 cups water

15g/½oz coarse salt

**For the lime butter dip**

90ml/6 tbsp dry white wine

90ml/6 tbsp white wine vinegar

3 shallots or 1 onion, finely chopped

225g/8oz/1 cup very cold unsalted (sweet) butter, cut into chunks

juice of 1 lime

salt and ground black pepper

lime wedges, to serve

**1** Wash the asparagus spears and trim the bases off evenly to give about 10cm/4in lengths. Bring a pan of water to the boil, add the salt then plunge in the asparagus. Cook for about 7 minutes or until you can just spear a stem with a knife and the blade slips out easily. Drain immediately and set aside, keeping the asparagus warm.

**2** A stainless steel pan with a handle is essential for the lime butter dip. If you are using a gas ring make sure the flame does not come round the side of the pan, as the sauce can burn easily. Combine the wine and vinegar in the pan with the shallots or onion, and simmer until the liquid has reduced to about 15ml/1 tbsp.

**3** Off the heat, vigorously whisk in the butter until the sauce thickens. Whisk in the lime juice until thoroughly combined. Taste the sauce and adjust the seasoning if necessary.

**4** Arrange ten asparagus spears per serving on warmed individual plates. Coarsely grind some black pepper over the top. Serve the warm lime butter dip in a bowl for handing round or in four small bowls.

### Cook's Tips
• There are two important points to remember when you add the butter to the sauce. Firstly, don't allow the sauce to boil. If the butter is taking a long time to melt, put the pan back over a gentle heat to speed it up. Secondly, you must not stop whisking until the butter is completely incorporated.
• You can use the asparagus trimmings to make soup or a lovely rich stock for stews or casseroles.

### Variations
This butter dip is a simple but effective sauce for shellfish. Variations include using cider instead of vinegar and orange or lemon juice instead of lime juice. Adding fish stock when reducing gives a strong fish flavour.

**Per portion** Energy 527kcal/2166kJ; Protein 7.8g; Carbohydrate 6.7g, of which sugars 6.1g; Fat 50.9g, of which saturates 31.5g; Cholesterol 128mg; Calcium 84mg; Fibre 4.5g; Sodium 1841mg.

# Lanark Blue and walnut salad

Lanark Blue is a blue cheese made from ewe's milk by Humphrey Errington on his farm near Biggar, south of Edinburgh. It is based on the French Roquefort but has a creamy texture and tangy flavour all its own. This is a delicious fresh-tasting first course but can be served without the figs as a cheese course.

**Serves 4**

mixed salad leaves

4 fresh figs

115g/4oz Lanark Blue, cut into small chunks

75g/3oz/¾ cup walnut halves

**For the dressing**

45ml/3 tbsp walnut oil

juice of 1 lemon

salt and ground black pepper

**1** Mix all the dressing ingredients together in a bowl. Whisk briskly until thick and emulsified.

**Cook's Tip**
Look for dark green salad leaves, such as lamb's lettuce and rocket (arugula), and reds, such as lollo rosso, as well as some crunchy leaves, such as Little Gem (Bibb), to add interest.

**Variation**
The figs may be replaced with ripe nectarines or peaches if you prefer. Wash and cut in half, discard the stone, then cut each half into three or four slices. If the skin is tough, you may need to remove it.

**2** Wash and dry the salad leaves then tear them gently into bitesize pieces. Place in a mixing bowl and toss with the dressing. Transfer to a large serving dish or divide among four individual plates, ensuring a good balance of colour and texture on each plate.

**3** Cut the figs into quarters and add to the salad leaves.

**4** Sprinkle the cheese over, crumbling it slightly. Then sprinkle over the walnuts, breaking them up roughly in your fingers as you go.

**Per portion** Energy 415kcal/1726kJ; Protein 10.6g; Carbohydrate 26.6g, of which sugars 26.4g; Fat 30.3g, of which saturates 7.3g; Cholesterol 22mg; Calcium 286mg; Fibre 4.5g; Sodium 383mg.

# Langoustines with garlic butter

There is nothing quite like the smell of garlic butter melting over shellfish. Freshly caught langoustines or jumbo shrimp are ideal for this simple yet extremely tasty first-course dish. Serve with plenty of fresh crusty white bread to soak up the delicious garlicky juices.

**Serves 4**

2 garlic cloves

5ml/1 tsp coarse salt

10ml/2 tsp chopped fresh flat leaf parsley, plus extra to garnish (optional)

250g/9oz/generous 1 cup butter, softened

juice of 2 lemons

pinch of cayenne pepper

20 freshly caught langoustines or Dublin Bay prawns (jumbo shrimp), cooked and peeled

ground black pepper

**1** Preheat the grill (broiler) to medium. Using a blender or food processor, blend the garlic cloves, salt and chopped parsley until quite well mixed. Then add the butter, lemon juice and cayenne pepper and blend again until all the ingredients are thoroughly combined.

**2** Scrape the butter mixture out of the food processor and into a bowl.

**3** Place the langoustines or prawns on a metal baking tray and put a blob of garlic butter on each one. Place under the preheated grill for about 5 minutes, or until the shellfish are cooked and the butter is bubbling.

**4** Lift five shellfish on to each plate and spoon over the collected pan juices. Serve immediately with a grind or two of black pepper and garnished with chopped fresh flat leaf parsley if you like. Accompany with fresh bread for mopping up the juices.

**Cook's Tip**
To cook the langoustines or prawns, plunge them into boiling water until the water returns to the boil and then drain and cool. Shell them by pulling off the head, legs and outer shell. Reserve a few heads to garnish, if you like.

Per portion Energy 616kcal/2552kJ; Protein 29.7g; Carbohydrate 4.9g, of which sugars 0.6g; Fat 53.3g, of which saturates 33.1g; Cholesterol 192mg; Calcium 68mg; Fibre 0.5g; Sodium 1098mg.

# Grilled oysters with Highland heather honey

Heather honey is very fragrant, the pollen gathered by bees late in the season when the heather on the moors is in full flower. Beekeepers in Scotland will take their hives up to the hills once the spring and early summer blossoms are over, so the flavour is more intense.

**Serves 4**

1 bunch spring onions (scallions), washed

20ml/4 tsp heather honey

10ml/2 tsp soy sauce

16 fresh oysters

**1** Preheat the grill (broiler) to medium. Chop the spring onions finely, removing any coarser outer leaves.

**2** Place the heather honey and soy sauce in a bowl and mix. Then add the finely chopped spring onions and mix them in thoroughly.

**3** Open the oysters with an oyster knife or a small, sharp knife, taking care to catch the liquid in a small bowl. Leave the oysters attached to one side of the shell. Strain the liquid to remove any pieces of broken shell, and set aside.

**4** Place a large teaspoon of the honey and spring onion mixture on top of each oyster.

**5** Place under the preheated grill until the mixture bubbles, which will take about 5 minutes. Take care when removing the oysters from the grill as the shells retain the heat. Make sure that you don't lose any of the sauce from inside the oyster shells.

**6** Allow the oysters to cool slightly before serving with slices of bread to soak up the juices. Either tip them straight into your mouth or lift them out with a spoon or fork.

Per portion Energy 81kcal/343kJ; Protein 9.2g; Carbohydrate 9.1g, of which sugars 6.9g; Fat 1.2g, of which saturates 0.2g; Cholesterol 46mg; Calcium 121mg; Fibre 0.3g; Sodium 588mg.

# Dressed crab with asparagus

Crab is a most flavoursome seafood, possibly better even than lobster and cheaper. This dish is a combination of two paragons: crab as the king of seafood and asparagus as a prince among vegetables.

**Serves 4**

24 asparagus spears

4 dressed crabs

30ml/2 tbsp mayonnaise

15ml/1 tbsp chopped fresh parsley

**1** Cook the asparagus as for Asparagus with Lime Butter Dip, but when cooked plunge the stems into iced water to stop them from cooking further. Drain them when cold and pat dry with kitchen paper.

**2** Scoop out the white crab meat from the shells and claws and place it in a bowl. If you can't find fresh crabs, you can use the same amount of canned or frozen white crab meat.

**3** Add the mayonnaise and chopped fresh parsley and combine with a fork. Place the mixture into the crab shells and add six asparagus spears per serving. Serve with crusty bread.

Per portion Energy 207kcal/859kJ; Protein 19.5g; Carbohydrate 3g, of which sugars 2.8g; Fat 13g, of which saturates 1.9g; Cholesterol 72mg; Calcium 157mg; Fibre 2.6g; Sodium 540mg.

# Sea trout mousse

This deliciously creamy mousse makes a little sea trout go a long way. It is equally good
made with other fish, like salmon or haddock, if sea trout is not available.

**Serves 6**

250g/9oz sea trout fillet

120ml/4fl oz/½ cup fish stock

2 gelatine leaves or 15ml/1 tbsp
powdered gelatine

juice of ½ lemon

30ml/2 tbsp dry sherry or dry
vermouth

30ml/2 tbsp freshly grated Parmesan

300ml/½ pint/1¼ cups
whipping cream

2 egg whites

15ml/1 tbsp sunflower oil

salt and ground white pepper

**For the garnish**

5cm/2in piece cucumber, with peel,
thinly sliced

6 small sprigs fresh dill or chervil,
plus extra, chopped

**3** Lightly whip the cream then fold it
into the cold trout mixture. Season to
taste, then cover with clear film (plastic
wrap) and chill until the mousse is
beginning to set.

**4** Beat the egg whites with a pinch of
salt until softly peaking. Stir one-third
into the trout mixture to lighten it, then
fold in the rest.

**1** Place the sea trout fillet in a shallow
pan. Pour in the fish stock and heat
to simmering point. Poach the fish for
about 3–4 minutes, until lightly cooked.
Lift the trout out and set it aside to cool
slightly. Strain the stock into a jug
(pitcher), then add the gelatine to the
hot stock and stir until dissolved
completely. Set aside to cool.

**2** When the trout is cool enough to
handle, remove the skin and flake the
flesh. Pour the stock into a food
processor. Process briefly, then gradually
add the flaked trout, lemon juice, sherry
or vermouth and Parmesan through the
feeder tube, continuing to process the
mixture until smooth. Scrape into a
large bowl and leave to cool completely.

**5** Lightly grease six ramekin dishes with
the sunflower oil. Divide the mousse
among the ramekins and level the
surface. Place in the refrigerator for 2–
3 hours, until set. Just before serving,
arrange a few slices of cucumber and a
small herb sprig on each mousse and
add a little chopped dill or chervil.

**Per portion** Energy 286kcal/1181kJ; Protein 12g; Carbohydrate 1.5g, of which sugars 1.5g; Fat 25.2g, of which saturates 13.9g; Cholesterol 58mg; Calcium 94mg; Fibre 0g; Sodium 111mg.

# Haddock and smoked salmon terrine

This substantial terrine makes a superb dish for a summer buffet, accompanied by dill mayonnaise and home-made bread and butter. Serve with a light, crisp salad.

**Serves 10–12 as a first course,**
**6–8 as a main course**

15ml/1 tbsp sunflower oil,
for greasing

350g/12oz oak-smoked salmon

900g/2lb haddock fillets, skinned

2 eggs, lightly beaten

105ml/7 tbsp crème fraîche

30ml/2 tbsp drained capers

30ml/2 tbsp drained soft green or
pink peppercorns

salt and ground white pepper

crème fraîche, peppercorns, fresh
dill and rocket (arugula), to garnish

**1** Preheat the oven to 200°C/400°F/ Gas 6. Grease a 1 litre/1¾ pint/4 cup loaf tin (pan) or terrine with the oil. Use half of the salmon to line the tin or terrine, letting some of the ends overhang the mould. Reserve the remaining smoked salmon.

**Variation**
Use any thick white fish fillets for this terrine – try halibut or Arctic bass. Cod is also good, although it is better to use a firm, chunky piece that will not crumble easily after being cooked. You could also use fresh salmon for a truly salmony flavour.

**2** Cut two long slices of haddock the length of the tin or terrine and set aside. Cut the rest of the haddock into small pieces. Season all the haddock.

**3** Combine the eggs, crème fraîche, capers and peppercorns in a bowl. Season, then stir in the small pieces of haddock. Spoon the mixture into the tin or terrine until one-third full. Smooth the surface with a spatula.

**4** Wrap the reserved long haddock fillets in the reserved smoked salmon. Lay them on top of the fish mixture in the tin or terrine.

**5** Fill the tin or terrine with the rest of the fish mixture, smooth the surface and fold the overhanging pieces of smoked salmon over the top. Cover tightly with a double thickness of foil. Tap the terrine to settle the contents.

**6** Stand the terrine in a roasting pan and pour in boiling water to come halfway up the sides. Place in the preheated oven and cook for 45 minutes–1 hour.

**7** Take the terrine out of the roasting pan, but do not remove the foil cover. Place two or three large heavy tins on the foil to weight it and leave until cold. Chill in the refrigerator for 24 hours.

**8** About 1 hour before serving, lift off the weights and remove the foil. Carefully invert the terrine on to a serving plate and lift off the terrine. Serve the terrine in thick slices with crème fraîche, peppercorns, fronds of dill and rocket leaves.

**Per portion** Energy 187kcal/785kJ; Protein 27.5g; Carbohydrate 0.3g, of which sugars 0.2g; Fat 8.5g, of which saturates 3.7g; Cholesterol 95mg; Calcium 31mg; Fibre 0g; Sodium 735mg.

# Mallard pâté

Mallard ducks are shot during the game season, which in Scotland is during the winter months. This recipe needs two days to prepare, as the birds need to be briefly cooked and allowed to rest overnight before making the rest of the pâté.

**Serves 4**

2 young mallards

a little groundnut (peanut) oil

185g/6½oz streaky (fatty) bacon

300g/11oz wild duck livers

10ml/2 tsp salt

ground black pepper

pinch each of grated nutmeg, ground ginger and ground cloves

275ml/9fl oz/generous 1 cup double (heavy) cream

4 egg yolks

37.5ml/2½ tbsp brandy

50g/2oz/scant ⅓ cup sultanas (golden raisins)

**1** Preheat the oven to 240°C/475°F/Gas 9. Remove the legs from the ducks. Season the birds and sprinkle with oil. Roast in the preheated oven for 15 minutes then remove from the oven and leave to rest, overnight if possible.

**2** The next day, preheat the oven to 190°C/375°F/Gas 5. Put the bacon, livers, salt, pepper and spices into a blender and purée to a smooth cream.

**3** Add the cream, egg yolks and brandy, and purée for a further 30 seconds. Push the mixture through a sieve into a mixing bowl and add the sultanas.

**4** Remove the breasts from the ducks and skin them. Dice the meat finely then mix into the liver mixture.

**5** Put the mixture in a terrine, cover with foil and cook in the oven in a roasting pan of hot water for 40–50 minutes. The centre should be slightly wobbly. Cool then chill for at least 4 hours. Serve with toast.

Per portion Energy 771kcal/3203kJ; Protein 48.5g; Carbohydrate 9.8g, of which sugars 9.8g; Fat 59.3g, of which saturates 28.4g; Cholesterol 636mg; Calcium 81mg; Fibre 0.3g; Sodium 1782mg.

# Strawberry and smoked venison salad

The combination of strawberries, balsamic vinegar and smoked venison creates a perfect ménage à trois. The tang of the vinegar sets off the sweetness of the strawberries, which must be ripe, and adds a fruity contrast to the rich, dry, smoky venison.

**Serves 4**

12 ripe Scottish strawberries

2.5ml/½ tsp caster (superfine) sugar

5ml/1 tsp balsamic vinegar

8 thin slices of smoked venison

mixed salad leaves

**For the dressing**

10ml/2 tsp olive oil

5ml/1 tsp balsamic vinegar

splash of strawberry wine (optional)

salt and ground black pepper

**1** Slice the strawberries vertically into three or four pieces then place in a bowl with the sugar and balsamic vinegar. Leave for 30 minutes.

**Cook's Tips**
• Suitable salad leaves include lollo rosso for colour, rocket (arugula) and lamb's lettuce (corn salad) for a peppery flavour and colour, and Little Gem (Bibb) for crunch.
• The sugar brings out the moisture in the strawberries, which combines with the balsamic vinegar to creates a lovely shiny coat. Do not leave them to stand for too long as they can become tired looking, 30 minutes is about right.

**2** Meanwhile, make the dressing by placing the olive oil and balsamic vinegar in a small bowl and whisking them together with the wine, if you are using it. Add salt and ground black pepper to taste.

**3** Cut the smoked venison into little strips. Mix the salad leaves together then toss with the dressing. Distribute the salad leaves among four plates, sprinkle with the strawberries and venison and serve immediately.

**Per portion** Energy 116kcal/486kJ; Protein 11.6g; Carbohydrate 3.1g, of which sugars 3.1g; Fat 6.8g, of which saturates 1.2g; Cholesterol 25mg; Calcium 16mg; Fibre 0.6g; Sodium 31mg.

# Fish and shellfish

The sea, the loch and the river have always provided
the mainstay of the diet in the Highlands and Islands
of Scotland, where the rugged mountains provide
little in the way of food and nourishment. Salmon is
perhaps the king of Scottish fish, and the rivers are
renowned fishing centres for the best in leaping fresh
wild salmon. Some fishing villages up and down the
coasts and on the Islands still bring in a daily catch of
haddock, sea trout, lobsters, crabs and prawns.

# Clam stovies

Clams are now harvested in the lochs, especially in Loch Fyne where some of the best Scottish clams are grown on ropes. Limpets or cockles can also be used if you can buy them fresh or collect them yourself along the seashore.

**Serves 4**

2.5 litres/4 pints/10 cups clams

potatoes (see step 3)

oil, for greasing

chopped fresh flat leaf parsley, to garnish

50g/2oz/¼ cup butter

salt and ground black pepper

**1** Wash the clams and soak them overnight in fresh cold water. This will clean them out and get rid of any sand and other detritus.

**2** Preheat the oven to 190°C/375°F/ Gas 5. Put the clams into a large pan, cover with water and bring to the boil. Add a little salt then simmer until the shells open. Reserve the cooking liquor. Shell the clams, reserving a few whole.

**3** Weigh the shelled clams. You will need three times their weight in unpeeled potatoes.

**4** Peel and slice the potatoes thinly. Lightly oil the base and sides of a flameproof, ovenproof dish. Arrange a layer of potatoes in the base of the dish, add a layer of the clams and season with a little salt and ground black pepper. Repeat until the ingredients are all used, finishing with a layer of potatoes on top. Finally, season lightly.

**5** Pour in some of the reserved cooking liquor to come about halfway up the dish. Dot the top with the butter then cover with foil. Bring to the boil on the stove over a medium-high heat, then bake in the preheated oven for 2 hours until the top is golden brown.

**6** Serve hot, garnished with chopped fresh flat leaf parsley.

Per portion Energy 320kcal/1348kJ; Protein 17.3g; Carbohydrate 36.7g, of which sugars 3.3g; Fat 12.6g, of which saturates 7g; Cholesterol 57mg; Calcium 188mg; Fibre 2.9g; Sodium 262mg.

# Queenies with smoked Ayrshire bacon

This recipe uses the classic combination of scallops with bacon, but this time using princess scallops – known locally as "Queenies" – which are cooked with a flavoursome cured bacon known as smoked Ayrshire bacon.

**Serves 4**

6 rashers (strips) smoked Ayrshire bacon, cut into thin strips

5ml/1 tsp ground turmeric

28 princess scallops

1 sprig each of parsley and thyme

1 bay leaf

6 black peppercorns

150ml/¼ pint/⅔ cup dry white wine

75ml/2½fl oz/⅓ cup double (heavy) cream

30ml/2 tbsp chopped fresh chives, to garnish

**1** Using a pan with a close-fitting lid, fry the bacon in its own fat until well cooked and crisp. Remove the bacon.

**2** Reduce the heat, stir the turmeric into the juices and cook for 1–2 minutes.

**3** Add the scallops to the pan with the herbs and peppercorns. Carefully pour in the wine (it will steam) and then cover with the lid. The scallops will only take a few minutes to cook. Test them by removing a thick one and piercing with a sharp knife to see if they are soft. Once they are cooked, remove from the pan and keep warm.

**4** Stir in the cream and increase the heat to allow the sauce to simmer. This should be a light sauce; if it becomes too thick then add a little water.

**5** Serve the scallops in warmed bowls or on plates with the sauce ladled over. Sprinkle with the crisp bacon and garnish with chopped fresh chives.

**Per portion** Energy 353kcal/1476kJ; Protein 36.5g; Carbohydrate 4.8g, of which sugars 0.5g; Fat 18.4g, of which saturates 9.1g; Cholesterol 106mg; Calcium 51mg; Fibre 0g; Sodium 904mg.

# East Neuk lobster with wholegrain mustard and cream

The East Neuk of Fife is the "corner" of Fife on the east coast of Scotland, an area bounded by the sea almost all around. From Elie to St Andrews, there is a proliferation of fishing villages, which in their time provided the vast majority of jobs in the area. Today Pittenweem is the only real fishing port with its own fish and shellfish market.

**Serves 2**

1 lobster, approximately 500g/1¼lb

10ml/2 tsp butter

splash of whisky (grain not malt)

1 shallot or ½ onion, finely chopped

50g/2oz button (white) mushrooms

splash of white wine

175ml/6fl oz/¾ cup double (heavy) cream

5ml/1 tsp wholegrain mustard

10ml/2 tsp chopped fresh chervil and a little tarragon

60ml/4 tbsp breadcrumbs

50g/2oz/¼ cup butter, melted

salt and ground black pepper

**1** Cook the lobster in boiling salted water for about 7 minutes then set aside to cool.

**Cook's Tip**
You can use a precooked lobster or prepared lobster meat for this recipe if you prefer.

**2** Once cool, cut the lobster down the middle, top to bottom, and remove the intestines down the back.

**3** Remove the meat from the tail, taking care not to let it break into pieces.

**4** Cut the tail meat into slanted slices. Remove the meat from the claws, keeping it as whole as possible. Wash the two half-shells out and set aside.

**5** Heat a frying pan over a low heat, add the butter and wait for it to bubble. Gently add the lobster meat and colour lightly (don't overcook or it will dry out). Pour in the whisky. If you have a gas hob, allow the flames to get inside the pan to briefly flame the pieces and burn off the alcohol; if the hob is electric, don't worry as it isn't vital. Remove the lobster meat.

**6** Add the chopped shallot or onion and the mushrooms, and cook gently over a medium-low heat for a few minutes until soft and the onion or shallot is transparent. Add a little white wine, then the cream, and allow to simmer to reduce to a light coating texture. Then add the mustard and the chopped herbs and mix well. Season to taste with a little salt and freshly ground black pepper. Meanwhile preheat the grill (broiler) to high.

**7** Place the two lobster half-shells on the grill pan. Distribute the lobster meat evenly throughout the two half-shells and spoon the sauce over. Sprinkle with breadcrumbs, drizzle with melted butter and brown under the preheated grill. Serve immediately.

Per portion Energy 812kcal/3357kJ; Protein 23.6g; Carbohydrate 12g, of which sugars 3.7g; Fat 74.9g, of which saturates 46g; Cholesterol 287mg; Calcium 127mg; Fibre 0.9g; Sodium 580mg.

# Baked salmon with watercress sauce

The quintessential Scottish centrepiece, the whole baked salmon makes a stunning focal point for a buffet. Baking it in foil is easier than poaching and retains the melting quality. Decorating the fish with thin slices of cucumber adds to this Highland delight.

**Serves 6–8**

2–3kg/4½–6½lb salmon, cleaned, with head and tail left on

3–5 spring onions (scallions), thinly sliced

1 lemon, thinly sliced

1 cucumber, thinly sliced

salt and ground black pepper

sprigs of fresh dill, to garnish

lemon wedges, to serve

**For the sauce**

3 garlic cloves, chopped

200g/7oz watercress leaves, finely chopped

40g/1½oz/¾ cup finely chopped fresh tarragon

300g/11oz/1¼ cups mayonnaise

15–30ml/1–2 tbsp lemon juice

200g/7oz/scant 1 cup unsalted (sweet) butter

**1** Preheat the oven to 180°C/350°F/ Gas 4. Rinse the salmon and lay it on a large piece of foil. Stuff the fish with the sliced spring onions and lemon. Season with salt and black pepper.

**2** Loosely fold the foil around the fish and fold the edges over to seal. Bake in the preheated oven for about 1 hour.

**3** Remove the fish from the oven and leave it to stand, still wrapped in the foil, for about 15 minutes. Then gently unwrap the foil parcel and set the salmon aside to cool.

**4** When the fish has cooled, carefully lift it on to a large plate, still covered with lemon slices. Cover the fish tightly with clear film (plastic wrap) and chill for several hours in the refrigerator.

**5** Remove the lemon slices from the top of the fish. Use a blunt knife to lift up the edge of the skin and carefully peel the skin away from the flesh, avoiding tearing the flesh. Pull out any fins at the same time. Carefully turn the salmon over and repeat on the other side. Leave the head on for serving, if you wish. Discard the skin.

**Variation**
If you prefer to poach the fish rather than baking it, you will need to use a fish kettle. Place the salmon on the rack in the kettle. Cover the salmon completely with cold water, place the lid over to cover, and slowly bring to a simmer. Cook for 5–10 minutes per 450g/1lb until tender.

**6** To make the sauce, put the garlic, watercress, tarragon, mayonnaise and lemon juice in a food processor or bowl, and process or mix to combine.

**7** Melt the butter then add to the watercress mixture a little at a time, processing or stirring until the butter has been incorporated and the sauce is thick and smooth. Cover and chill.

**8** Arrange the cucumber slices in overlapping rows along the length of the fish, so that they look like large fish scales. You can also slice the cucumber diagonally to produce longer slices for decoration. Trim the edges with scissors. Serve the fish, garnished with dill and lemon wedges, with the watercress sauce alongside.

**Cook's Tip**
Do not prepare the sauce more than a few hours ahead of serving as the watercress will discolour.

**Per portion** Energy 1044kcal/4323kJ; Protein 51.6g; Carbohydrate 1.4g, of which sugars 1.2g; Fat 92.4g, of which saturates 28.5g; Cholesterol 231mg; Calcium 135mg; Fibre 0.7g; Sodium 558mg.

# Salmon with herb butter

A delicious fish with a delicate flavour, salmon needs to be served simply. Here, fresh dill
and lemon are combined to make a slightly piquant butter.

**2** Spoon the butter on to a piece
of baking parchment and roll up,
smoothing with your hands into a
sausage shape. Twist the ends tightly,
wrap in clear film (plastic wrap) and put
in the freezer for 20 minutes, until firm.

**3** Meanwhile, preheat the oven to
190°C/375°F/Gas 5. Cut out four
squares of foil to encase the salmon
steaks and grease with butter. Place a
salmon steaks into the centre of each.

**4** Remove the herb butter from the
freezer and slice into eight rounds.
Place two rounds on top of each
salmon steak with a halved lemon slice
in the centre and a sprig of dill on top.
Lift up the edges of the foil and crinkle
them together until well sealed. Place
on a baking tray.

**Serves 4**

50g/2oz/¼ cup butter, softened, plus
extra for greasing

finely grated rind of 1 lemon

15ml/1 tbsp lemon juice

15ml/1 tbsp chopped fresh dill

4 salmon steaks

2 lemon slices, halved

4 sprigs of fresh dill

salt and ground black pepper

**1** Place the butter, lemon rind, lemon
juice and chopped fresh dill in a small
bowl and mix together with a fork until
blended. Season to taste with salt and
ground black pepper.

**5** Bake for 20 minutes. Place the
unopened parcels on warmed plates.
Open the parcels and slide the contents
on to the plates with the juices.

**Per portion** Energy 409kcal/1700kJ; Protein 35.6g; Carbohydrate 0.2g, of which sugars 0.2g; Fat 29.6g, of which saturates 9.8g; Cholesterol 114mg; Calcium 47mg; Fibre 0.2g; Sodium 156mg.

# Quenelles of sole

Traditionally, these light fish "dumplings" are made with pike, but they are even better made with sole or other white fish. They make a great lunchtime meal or late-night supper, with bread and a crisp salad.

**Serves 6**

450g/1lb sole fillets, skinned and cut into large pieces

4 egg whites

600ml/1 pint/2½ cups double (heavy) cream

freshly grated nutmeg

salt and ground black pepper

chopped fresh parsley, to garnish

**For the sauce**

1 small shallot, finely chopped

60ml/4 tbsp dry vermouth

120ml/4fl oz/½ cup fish stock

150ml/¼ pint/⅔ cup double (heavy) cream

50g/2oz/¼ cup butter, diced

**2** Whip the cream until very thick, but not stiff. Gradually fold it into the fish mixture. Season, then stir in nutmeg to taste. Cover the bowl and refrigerate for several hours.

**3** To make the sauce, combine the shallot, vermouth and fish stock in a small pan. Bring to the boil and cook until reduced by half. Add the cream and boil until it has a thick consistency.

**4** Strain and return to the pan. Whisk in the butter, one piece at a time, until the sauce is creamy. Season and keep hot, but do not allow to boil.

**5** Bring a wide shallow pan of lightly salted water to the boil, then reduce the heat so that the water surface barely trembles. Using two tablespoons dipped in hot water, shape the fish mousse into ovals. As each quenelle is shaped, slip it into the simmering water.

**6** Poach the quenelles in batches for 8–10 minutes, until just firm to the touch but still slightly creamy inside. Lift out using a slotted spoon, drain on kitchen paper and keep hot. When all the quenelles are cooked, arrange them on warmed plates. Pour the sauce around, garnish with parsley and serve.

**1** Check the sole for stray bones, then put the pieces in a food processor. Season. Switch the machine on and, with the motor running, add the egg whites one at a time through the feeder tube to make a smooth purée. Press the purée through a metal sieve placed over a bowl. Stand the bowl of purée in a larger bowl and surround it with plenty of crushed ice or ice cubes.

**Per portion** Energy 771kcal/3180kJ; Protein 17.7g; Carbohydrate 3.3g, of which sugars 3g; Fat 75.4g, of which saturates 46.1g; Cholesterol 227mg; Calcium 89mg; Fibre 0.1g; Sodium 195mg.

# Herrings in oatmeal

Herrings have a wonderfully strong flavour and are ideal for simple recipes. Traditional to the Northern Isles and the east coast, these herrings coated in oats make for hearty meals, and are also easy to prepare and cook.

**Serves 4**

175ml/6fl oz/¾ cup thick mayonnaise

15ml/1 tbsp Dijon mustard

7.5ml/1½ tsp tarragon vinegar

4 herrings, approximately 225g/8oz each

juice of 1 lemon

115g/4oz/generous 1 cup medium rolled oats

salt and ground black pepper

**1** Place the mayonnaise in a small mixing bowl and add the mustard and vinegar. Mix thoroughly and then chill for a few minutes.

**2** Place one fish at a time on a chopping board, cut side down, and open out. Press gently along the backbone with your thumbs. Turn the fish over and carefully lift away the backbone.

**3** Squeeze lemon juice over both sides of the fish, then season with salt and ground black pepper. Fold the fish in half, skin side outwards.

**4** Preheat the grill (broiler) to medium hot. Place the rolled oats on a plate then coat each herring evenly in the oats, pressing it in gently.

**5** Place the herrings on a grill rack and grill (broil) the fish for 3–4 minutes on each side, until the skin is golden brown and crisp and the flesh flakes easily when the fish is cut into. Serve immediately on warmed plates with the mustard sauce handed round in a separate dish or bowl.

**Per portion** Energy 755kcal/3143kJ; Protein 36.7g; Carbohydrate 32.6g, of which sugars 0.6g; Fat 54g, of which saturates 9.3g; Cholesterol 98mg; Calcium 149mg; Fibre 3g; Sodium 459mg.

# Mackerel with gooseberry relish

Off Scotland's west coast it is still possible to fish for mackerel yourself and quite often at the weekends part-time fishermen can be found selling fresh mackerel at the harbours. Mackerel is very good for you, and the tart gooseberries give you a serving of fruit too.

**Serves 4**

4 whole mackerel

60ml/4 tbsp olive oil

**For the sauce**

250g/9oz gooseberries

25g/1oz/2 tbsp soft light brown sugar

5ml/1 tsp wholegrain mustard

salt and ground black pepper

**1** For the sauce, wash and trim the gooseberries and then roughly chop them, so there are some pieces larger than others.

**2** Cook the gooseberries in a little water with the sugar in a small pan. A thick and chunky purée will form. Add the mustard and season to taste with salt and ground black pepper.

**Cook's Tips**
• Turn the grill (broiler) on well in advance as the fish need a fierce heat to cook quickly. If you like the fish but hate the smell, try barbecuing outside.
• The foil lining in the grill pan is to catch the smelly drips. Simply roll it up and throw it away afterwards, leaving a nice clean grill pan.

**3** Preheat the grill (broiler) to high and line the grill pan with foil. Using a sharp knife, slash the fish two or three times down each side then season and brush with the olive oil.

**4** Place the fish in the grill pan and grill (broil) for about 4 minutes on each side until cooked. You may need to cook them for a few minutes longer if they are particularly large. The slashes will open up to speed cooking and the skin should be lightly browned. To check that they are cooked properly, use a small sharp knife to pierce the skin and check for uncooked flesh.

**5** Place the mackerel on warmed plates and spread generous dollops of the gooseberry relish over them. Pass the remaining sauce around at the table.

**Per portion** Energy 576kcal/2390kJ; Protein 38.1g; Carbohydrate 8.4g, of which sugars 8.4g; Fat 43.5g, of which saturates 8.2g; Cholesterol 108mg; Calcium 43mg; Fibre 1.5g; Sodium 128mg.

# Pale smoked haddock flan

The classic combination of potatoes and smoked fish is reworked in pastry. Always ask your fishmonger for "pale" smoked rather than "yellow" haddock as the latter tends to have been dyed to look bright and often has not been smoked properly at all.

**Serves 4**

**For the pastry**

225g/8oz/2 cups plain (all-purpose) flour

pinch of salt

115g/4oz/1½ cup cold butter, cut into chunks

cold water, to mix

**For the filling**

2 pale smoked haddock fillets (approximately 200g/7oz)

600ml/1 pint/2½ cups full-fat (whole) milk

3–4 black peppercorns

sprig of fresh thyme

150ml/¼ pint/⅔ cup double (heavy) cream

2 eggs

200g/7oz potatoes, peeled and diced

ground black pepper

**1** Preheat the oven to 200°C/400°F/ Gas 6. Use a food processor to make the pastry. Put the flour, salt and butter into the food processor bowl and process until the mixture resembles fine breadcrumbs. Pour in a little cold water (you will need about 40ml/8 tsp but see Cook's Tip) and continue to process until the mixture forms a ball. If this takes longer than 30 seconds add a dash or two more water. Take the pastry ball out of the food processor, wrap in clear film (plastic wrap) and leave to rest in a cool place for about 30 minutes.

**2** Roll out the dough and use to line a 20cm/8in flan tin (quiche pan). Prick the base of the pastry all over with a fork then bake blind in the preheated oven for 20 minutes.

**3** Put the haddock in a pan with the milk, peppercorns and thyme. Poach for 10 minutes. Remove the fish from the pan and flake into small chunks. Allow the poaching liquor to cool.

**4** Whisk the cream and eggs together thoroughly, then whisk in the cooled poaching liquid.

**5** Layer the flan case with the flaked fish and diced potato, seasoning with black pepper.

**6** Pour the cream mixture over the top. Put the flan in the oven and bake for 40 minutes, until lightly browned on top and set.

**Cook's Tip**

Different flours absorb water at different rates. A traditional rule of thumb is to use the same number of teaspoons of water as the number of ounces of flour, but some flours will require less water and others more, so add the water gradually. If you add too much water, the pastry will become unworkable and you will need to add more flour.

**Variation**

This recipe is also delicious if you add hard boiled eggs, chopped into quarters or eighths before adding the potatoes.

Per portion Energy 734kcal/3064kJ; Protein 23.8g; Carbohydrate 58.4g, of which sugars 8.2g; Fat 46.8g, of which saturates 27.9g; Cholesterol 225mg; Calcium 280mg; Fibre 2.3g; Sodium 636mg.

# Meat, venison, poultry and game

Central to the traditional Scottish way of life, meat, venison, poultry and game have always played a key role. Scottish beef is renowned throughout the world for the natural way it is reared. Lamb and pork dishes are also enjoyed, especially in the Lowlands. Traditional favourites like haggis are still widely made. Poultry was reared in the back yard of every home and croft, from chickens and hens to ducks and geese, all providing eggs every day and a roast for special occasions. Game – from pheasant to rabbit – was available to rich and poor alike. The Highlands and glens teemed with wild birds ready to be taken home, plucked or skinned and made into a glorious banquet.

# Griddled loin of lamb with barley risotto

A loin of lamb is taken from the back or the saddle, and it should be completely clear of fat or gristle so you are getting pure meat. Good lamb needs little cooking – remember to take it out of the refrigerator well before you cook it to raise it to room temperature as it will then cook more quickly. Always pat the meat dry before putting it on a griddle pan.

**Serves 4**

a little olive oil

750ml/1¼ pints/3 cups chicken stock

75g/3oz/6 tbsp butter

1 onion, finely chopped

225g/8oz/1 cup barley

50g/2oz Bonnet cheese

3 loins of lamb

salt and ground black pepper

virgin olive oil, to serve

**1** Prepare a cast-iron ridged griddle or heavy pan by brushing it with olive oil. Bring the stock to the boil. Melt the butter in a pan, and sweat the onion.

**2** Add the barley to the pan and stir to coat well with the olive oil.

**3** Add about one-third of the stock. Bring to the boil then reduce the heat, stirring all the time until the liquid is absorbed by the barley. Add half of the remaining stock and continue to stir and absorb. Finally add the rest of the stock, stirring all the time. You will create a thick, creamy mixture, with the barley still having a little "bite" to it. You may need more or less liquid depending on the barley; if you need more just add boiling water.

**4** Grate the cheese and add to the barley when it has absorbed all the stock. Stir in well, season with salt and ground black pepper, and keep warm.

**5** Heat the griddle or heavy pan until very hot. Brush the lamb with olive oil and season with salt and pepper. Sear the lamb quickly all over to brown it, then reduce the heat and cook for a further 8 minutes, turning occasionally. Leave it in a warm place to rest for 5 minutes.

**6** Serve by carving thickish slices from each loin at an angle. You should get four slices from each loin, giving three per person. Add a splash of virgin olive oil to the risotto, place a mound of risotto on each warmed plate and prop the slices of lamb on it.

**Per portion** Energy 827kcal/3460kJ; Protein 49.8g; Carbohydrate 53.2g, of which sugars 2.2g; Fat 47.7g, of which saturates 25.2g; Cholesterol 223mg; Calcium 55mg; Fibre 0.5g; Sodium 348mg.

# Braised shoulder of lamb with dulse

Dulse is a sea vegetable or seaweed and is used traditionally for flavouring dishes, especially lamb and mutton. On the Outer Hebrides the sheep will graze near the seashore and will actually eat the seaweed as well. Soay sheep, a hardy breed, feed almost exclusively on it and the flavour of their meat is improved by it too.

**Serves 4**

1.8kg/4lb shoulder of lamb, bone in and well trimmed of fat

30ml/2 tbsp vegetable oil

250g/9oz onions

25g/1oz/2 tbsp butter

pinch of caster (superfine) sugar

500ml/scant pint water

50g/2oz dried dulse

1 bay leaf

salt and ground black pepper

**1** Preheat the oven to 180°C/350°F/ Gas 4, if necessary (see Step 5). Season the lamb all over.

**2** Place a pan, big enough to hold the lamb and with a lid, on the stove. When hot, add the oil and brown the lamb all over. This can be a little difficult, as there are bits you really can't reach with the bone in, but brown as much as you can.

**Cook's Tip**
Press the onion hard through the sieve when straining the sauce, and if it is a bit thin boil it for a short while to reduce slightly.

**3** Remove the lamb from the pan and drain off the excess fat, reserving it in case you need extra for the sauce. Peel the onions, cut in half and slice – not too finely – into half rounds.

**4** Return the pan to a medium heat and add the butter. When it has melted completely, add the sliced onions with the sugar and a little salt and ground black pepper. Stir to coat with the butter then colour, without burning, for about 9 minutes.

**5** Place the lamb on top of the onions, add the water, dulse and bay leaf, and season again. Cover and bring to the boil. Cook for 2 hours either over a very low heat or in the oven if the pan will fit and has ovenproof handles.

**6** Remove the lamb from the pan, set aside and keep warm. Check the sauce for consistency, adding some of the reserved fat if necessary. Strain and adjust the seasoning. Slice the lamb and serve with the sauce.

**Per portion** Energy 677kcal/2808kJ; Protein 43.5g; Carbohydrate 5.2g, of which sugars 3.7g; Fat 53.7g, of which saturates 23.7g; Cholesterol 194mg; Calcium 48mg; Fibre 1.3g; Sodium 188mg.

# Haggis, potato and apple tart

Haggis is probably the best known of all Scottish traditional dishes. It is still widely enjoyed today, although it is more frequently bought ready-made than prepared by hand in the home. Apple combines very well with haggis as its tart and sweet taste cuts through the richness of the meat.

**3** Place the smaller pastry disc on a baking tray and spread half the potatoes over it, leaving a rim of about 2cm/¾in all the way round.

**4** Cut the haggis open and crumble the meat on top. Slice the apple into circles and spread all over the haggis. Then top with the rest of the potatoes.

**5** Brush the egg all around the exposed pastry rim then place the other pastry circle on top, pushing down on the rim to seal. Use a fork to tidy up the edges and then press down around the edge again to create a firm seal. Leave to rest for 10 minutes.

**6** Brush over with more egg and bake the tart in the preheated oven for 10 minutes to set the pastry. Then reduce the oven temperature to 200°C/400°F/Gas 6 and bake for a further 40 minutes until evenly browned and cooked. Serve in slices.

**Serves 4**

450g/1lb peeled potatoes, sliced

1 garlic clove, crushed with 1 tsp salt

freshly grated nutmeg

400g/14oz ready-made puff pastry

300g/11oz haggis

2 cooking apples, cored

1 egg, beaten

salt and ground black pepper

**1** Preheat the oven to 220°C/425°F/Gas 7. Slice the potatoes and mix with the crushed garlic. Season with a little freshly grated nutmeg and salt and ground black pepper.

**2** Roll out the puff pastry into two discs, one about 25cm/10in in diameter and the other a little larger.

Haggis is usually made of mutton and lamb and their offal, highly spiced and bound together with oatmeal, and packed into a sheep's stomach ready for lengthy boiling. Haggis is generally sold cooked, ready for further cooking and reheating.

**Per portion** Energy 698kcal/2919kJ; Protein 15.8g; Carbohydrate 72.9g, of which sugars 6.1g; Fat 41.2g, of which saturates 5.8g; Cholesterol 68mg; Calcium 88mg; Fibre 1.9g; Sodium 901mg.

# Angus pasties

Aberdeen Angus beef is the traditional filling for pasties, as it is such a well-known breed, but any really good-quality beef may be used. These pasties are perfect served either cold or warmed for lunch or as a snack, and make great picnic food.

**Makes 10**

**For the pastry**

900g/2lb/8 cups plain (all-purpose) flour

225g/8oz/1 cup butter

225g/8oz/1cup lard or white cooking fat

pinch of salt

**For the filling**

1.2kg/2½lb rump (round) steak

225g/8oz/1¾ cups beef suet (US chilled, grated shortening)

5 onions, finely chopped

salt and ground black pepper

**1** Preheat the oven to 200°C/400°F/ Gas 6. Using a mixer, place the flour in the mixing bowl and blend in the butter and lard or white cooking fat using the dough hook. Add salt and mix to a stiff dough, adding water gradually as needed. Leave the pastry ball to rest in clear film (plastic wrap) for 30 minutes.

**2** Meanwhile, trim the meat of any excess fat and cut into 1cm/½in squares. Chop the suet finely then mix with the meat and onions. Season.

**3** Divide the pastry into ten equal sized pieces. Roll out each piece into an oval, not too thinly, and divide the meat mixture among them at one end, leaving an edge for sealing. Dampen the edges of each oval with cold water and fold the pastry over the filling.

**4** Seal carefully – use a fork to make sure the edges are stuck together securely. Make a hole in the top of each pasty. Place on a greased baking sheet and bake in the preheated oven for 45 minutes. Serve hot, or allow to cool and refrigerate.

**Per portion** Energy 1131kcal/4714kJ; Protein 37.7g; Carbohydrate 84.8g, of which sugars 4.5g; Fat 74.5g, of which saturates 37.9g; Cholesterol 171mg; Calcium 162mg; Fibre 3.9g; Sodium 232mg.

# Roast fillet of beef with wild garlic sauce

Perhaps the most magnificent of Scottish dishes is the fillet steak, cooked to perfection and served with a luxurious sauce. Wild garlic, also known as ramsons, grows all over Britain, Europe and Scandinavia, though unfortunately not elsewhere (see Variation for alternatives). The aroma is unmistakable and can be smelt from a distance – very garlicky.

**Serves 4**

4 fillet steaks (beef tenderloin)

15ml/1 tbsp olive oil

5ml/1 tsp butter

15ml/1 tbsp dry white wine

2 egg yolks

250g/9oz/generous 1 cup butter, melted

20 wild garlic leaves

squeeze of lemon juice (optional)

salt and ground black pepper

**1** Dry the steaks using kitchen paper and set aside.

**2** Heat a heavy pan with a good handle then add the oil and butter. Just as the butter is bubbling up, place the steaks in the pan. Keep the pan hot and brown the meat all over to seal in the juices, then reduce the heat to cook the meat to whatever stage of pinkness you want; 6 minutes will make them medium rare.

**3** Remove the steaks from the pan and keep warm between two plates.

**4** Allow the pan to cool for a few minutes then pour in the wine. If it bubbles up as you pour it in, wait for the pan to cool a little more before pouring in the rest.

**5** Whisk the egg yolks until smooth and blended, then whisk them into the wine over a low heat, taking care that they don't scramble. They should foam and thicken slightly. Remove them from the heat if they begin to firm up.

**Variation**
If you are finding it hard to get fresh wild garlic, or it is out of season, you can use a garlic clove instead, chopped finely and added at the end in the same way as the leaves. For a richer flavour, roast a bulb of garlic in its skin and scoop out the flesh to flavour the sauce. Add a finely sliced wild leek or onion to the sauce to provide a lovely texture and to enhance the flavour.

**6** Then, off the heat, slowly pour in the melted butter, a little bit to start with, whisking all the time. (You may not wish to add all the whey from the butter as it tends to make the sauce less thick.) This is where the handle comes in, and putting the pan on a damp cloth will help to stop it from moving about.

**7** Rinse the wild garlic leaves thoroughly and drain on kitchen paper. Shred them finely and stir gently into the sauce. Season to taste with salt and ground black pepper. If you want a sharper taste, add a squeeze or two of fresh lemon juice.

**8** Using prewarmed plates, place one steak on each, in the centre. Then spoon the wild garlic sauce over the top, letting it spill over on to the side of the plate. Serve with roast potatoes and steamed vegetables.

**Per portion** Energy 744kcal/3076kJ; Protein 33.8g; Carbohydrate 0.6g, of which sugars 0.6g; Fat 67.1g, of which saturates 38.6g; Cholesterol 328mg; Calcium 42mg; Fibre 0.3g; Sodium 459mg.

# Beef stew with oysters and Belhaven beer

Oysters have been collected from the waters south of Edinburgh since Roman times. They were very cheap and readily available in the 18th and 19th centuries, with "oyster lassies" wandering through the streets of Edinburgh selling them, calling their familiar cry, "Wha'll o' caller ou?" – "Who will have fresh oysters?"

**Serves 4**

1kg/2¼lb rump (round) steak

6 thin rashers (strips) streaky (fatty) bacon

12 oysters

50g/2oz/½ cup plain (all-purpose) flour

generous pinch of cayenne pepper

butter or olive oil, for greasing

3 shallots, finely chopped

300ml/½ pint/1¼ cups Belhaven Best beer

salt and ground black pepper

**1** Preheat the oven to 180°C/350°F/ Gas 4. You need thin strips of beef for this recipe, so place the steaks one at a time between sheets of clear film (plastic wrap) and beat it with a rolling pin until it is flattened and thin. Slice the meat into 24 thin strips, wide enough to roll around an oyster.

**2** Stretch the bacon rashers lengthways by placing them on a chopping board and, holding one end down with your thumb, pulling them out using the thick side of a sharp knife. Cut each rasher into four pieces.

**3** Remove the oysters from their shells, retaining the liquid from inside their shells in a separate container. Set aside.

**4** Cut each oyster in half lengthways and roll each piece in a strip of bacon, ensuring that the bacon goes around at least once and preferably covers the oyster at each end. Then roll in a strip of beef so no oyster is visible.

**5** Season the flour with the cayenne pepper and salt and black pepper, then roll the meat in it.

**6** Lightly grease a large flameproof casserole with butter or olive oil. Sprinkle the shallots evenly over the base. Place the floured meat rolls on top, evenly spaced.

**7** Slowly pour over the beer, bring to the boil then cover and cook in the oven for 1½–2 hours.

**8** The flour from around the meat will have thickened the stew sauce and produced a lovely rich gravy. Serve with creamy mashed potatoes and fresh steamed vegetables.

**Cook's Tip**
To open the oysters use an oyster knife, grasping the oyster in your other hand with a dish towel. If you don't have an oyster knife, use a small knife or a pen knife, although you should be careful of cutting yourself as the blade can easily slip.

**Variation**
Belhaven Best, beautifully honey coloured, is a draught (draft) ale. You could substitute your favourite ale or even Guinness if you prefer. If you want to create the dish without beer, use a good beef stock. Half a glass of red wine would also make a good addition if you are using stock.

**Per portion** Energy 528kcal/2208kJ; Protein 61.4g; Carbohydrate 12.7g, of which sugars 2.5g; Fat 24.4g, of which saturates 10.1g; Cholesterol 182mg; Calcium 52mg; Fibre 0.6g; Sodium 634mg.

# Smoked venison with garlic mashed potatoes

Smoked venison is one of Scotland's lesser known treasures, and it can be used in many different ways. The best smoked venison is, of course, from wild animals taken from the moors and hills. The only smoker in Scotland to smoke wild venison is Rannoch Smokery in Perthshire. This warming dish makes an ideal supper or lunch.

**Serves 4**

675g/1½lb peeled potatoes

175ml/6fl oz/¾ cup milk

1 garlic clove

10ml/2 tsp sea salt

olive oil, for greasing and to serve

75ml/2½fl oz/⅓ cup double (heavy) cream

115g/4oz sliced smoked venison

salad leaves, to garnish

**1** Preheat the oven to 180°C/350°F/ Gas 4. Slice the potatoes thinly using a sharp knife or mandolin. Place in a pan and pour in the milk.

**2** Crush the garlic with the sea salt using the side of a knife. Stir the mixture into the potatoes. Bring to the boil over a gentle heat, stirring occasionally, until the starch comes out of the potatoes and the milk begins to thicken.

**3** Grease the inside of a large gratin dish with a little olive oil.

**4** Add the cream to the potatoes and, stirring gently so the potatoes don't break up, combine well. Allow to just come to the boil again then pour the mixture carefully into the ovenproof gratin dish.

**5** Place the dish in the preheated oven for about 1 hour until lightly browned and tender.

**6** To serve, scoop the potato on to warmed plates and put a pile of smoked venison on top, adding a splash of olive oil over each serving. Garnish with salad leaves.

**Cook's Tips**
• Use good tasty potatoes, such as King Edward or Maris Piper, for this dish (US russet or Idaho).
• If you are feeling generous, you could use more smoked venison.

**Per portion** Energy 281kcal/1180kJ; Protein 15.6g; Carbohydrate 29.5g, of which sugars 4.5g; Fat 12g, of which saturates 6.1g; Cholesterol 25mg; Calcium 80mg; Fibre 1.7g; Sodium 1050mg.

# Venison stew

This simple yet deeply flavoured stew makes a wonderful supper dish, incorporating rich red wine and sweet redcurrant jelly with the depth of the bacon. Venison is popular in Scotland but you could substitute good-quality beef, if you prefer. Venison is a very lean meat, so bacon is included in this dish to provide some fat for the sauce.

**Serves 4**

1.3kg/3lb stewing venison
(shoulder or topside), trimmed
and diced

50g/2oz/¼ cup butter

225g/8oz piece of streaky
(fatty) bacon, cut into
2cm/¾in lardons

2 large onions, chopped

1 large carrot, peeled
and diced

1 large garlic clove, crushed

30ml/2 tbsp plain
(all-purpose) flour

½ bottle red wine

dark stock (see Step 4)

1 bay leaf

sprig of fresh thyme

200g/7oz button (white)
mushrooms, sliced

30ml/2 tbsp redcurrant jelly

salt and ground black pepper

**1** Dry the venison thoroughly using kitchen paper. Set to one side.

**2** Melt the butter in a large, heavy pan then brown the bacon lardons over a medium-high heat, stirring occasionally. Reduce the heat slightly to medium and add the onions and carrot, stir in and brown lightly.

**3** Add the venison to the pan along with the garlic and stir into the mixture. Sprinkle on the flour and mix well.

**4** Pour in the wine and dark stock to cover, along with the herbs, mushrooms and redcurrant jelly.

**5** Cover the pan and simmer over a low heat until the meat is cooked, approximately 1½–2 hours. Serve immediately with creamy mashed potato and green vegetables of your choice.

**Cook's Tip**
This dish can be cooked and then left until required – a couple of days if need be. The flavours will be enhanced if it has been left for a while. Simply reheat and serve when needed.

**Per portion** Energy 727kcal/3045kJ; Protein 83.8g; Carbohydrate 17.5g, of which sugars 14.4g; Fat 31.3g, of which saturates 13.8g; Cholesterol 226mg; Calcium 70mg; Fibre 2.9g; Sodium 985mg.

# Venison pie

This is a variation on cottage or shepherd's pie and the result, using rich venison, is particularly tasty – a hearty treat after an energetic day hiking through the Highlands. Serve with lightly steamed green vegetables such as kale or cabbage.

**Serves 6**

30ml/2 tbsp olive oil

2 leeks, washed, trimmed and chopped

1kg/2¼lb minced (ground) venison

30ml/2 tbsp chopped fresh parsley

300ml/½ pint/1¼ cups game consommé

salt and ground black pepper

**For the topping**

1.4kg/3¼lb mixed root vegetables, such as sweet potatoes, parsnips and swede (rutabaga), coarsely chopped

15ml/1 tbsp horseradish sauce

25g/1oz/2 tbsp butter

**1** Heat the oil in a pan over a medium heat. Add the leeks and cook for about 8 minutes, or until they are softened and beginning to brown.

**2** Add the minced venison to the pan and cook over a medium heat, stirring frequently, for about 10 minutes or until the venison is thoroughly browned all over.

**3** Add the chopped fresh parsley and stir it in thoroughly, then add the consommé and salt and ground black pepper. Stir well. Bring the mixture to the boil over a medium heat, then reduce the heat to low, cover and simmer gently for about 20 minutes, stirring occasionally.

**4** Meanwhile, preheat the oven to 200°C/400°F/Gas 6 and prepare the pie topping. Cook the chopped root vegetables in boiling salted water to cover for 15–20 minutes.

**Variation**
This pie can be made with other minced (ground) meats, such as beef, lamb or pork. You may need to adapt the cooking times for these, depending on the type and quantity that you use, although the basic recipe remains the same. You can also use other types of game meats for this pie, such as finely chopped or minced rabbit or hare.

**5** Drain the vegetables and put them in a bowl. Mash them together with the horseradish sauce, butter and plenty of ground black pepper.

**6** Spoon the venison mixture into a large ovenproof dish and cover the top evenly with the mashed vegetables. It is often easier to spoon it over in small quantities rather than pouring it on and then smoothing it out.

**7** Bake in the preheated oven for 20 minutes, or until piping hot and beginning to brown. Serve immediately, with steamed green vegetables.

**Cook's Tip**
• Use wild venison if possible as it has the best flavour and the lowest fat. If you can't get it, then use farmed venison, which will work well in this dish. Look for organic farmed vension.
• If leeks aren't available, then use a large onion and chop it coarsely.

**Per portion** Energy 307kcal/1291kJ; Protein 39.8g; Carbohydrate 13.2g, of which sugars 12.5g; Fat 12g, of which saturates 4.1g; Cholesterol 93mg; Calcium 154mg; Fibre 5.8g; Sodium 176mg.

# Stoved chicken

The word "stoved" is derived from the French *étuver* – to cook in a covered pot – and originates from the time of the Franco/Scottish Alliance in the 17th century. Instead of buying chicken joints, you can also choose either chicken thighs or chicken drumsticks.

**Serves 4**

900g/2lb potatoes, cut into 5mm/¼in slices

2 large onions, thinly sliced

15ml/1 tbsp chopped fresh thyme

25g/1oz/ 2 tbsp butter

15ml/1 tbsp oil

2 large bacon rashers (strips), chopped

4 large chicken joints, halved

1 bay leaf

600ml/1 pint/2½ cups chicken stock

salt and ground black pepper

**1** Preheat the oven to 150°C/300°F/ Gas 2. Make a thick layer of half the potato slices in the base of a large, heavy casserole, then cover with half the onion. Sprinkle with half the thyme and salt and ground black pepper.

**2** Heat the butter and oil in a large frying pan then brown the bacon and chicken. Using a slotted spoon, transfer the chicken and bacon to the casserole. Reserve the fat in the pan.

**3** Tuck the bay leaf in between the chicken. Sprinkle the remaining thyme over, then cover with the remaining onion, followed by a neat layer of overlapping potato slices. Season.

**4** Pour the stock into the casserole. Brush the top layer of the sliced potatoes with the reserved fat from the frying pan, then cover tightly and cook in the preheated oven for about 2 hours, until the chicken is thoroughly cooked and tender.

**5** Preheat the grill (broiler) to high. Uncover the casserole and place under the grill and cook until the slices of potato are beginning to brown and crisp. Serve hot.

**Variation**
You can use tarragon instead of the thyme: French tarragon has a superior flavour to the Russian variety.

Per portion Energy 630kcal/2653kJ; Protein 69.2g; Carbohydrate 48.2g, of which sugars 8.9g; Fat 19.2g, of which saturates 7.2g; Cholesterol 195mg; Calcium 57mg; Fibre 3.9g; Sodium 574mg.

# Hunter's chicken

This tasty dish sometimes has strips of green pepper in the sauce instead of the mushrooms. It is excellent served with creamy mashed potatoes, and can be great for a lunch or late supper with a good chunk of fresh crusty bread.

**Serves 4**

30ml/2 tbsp olive oil

15g/½oz/1 tbsp butter

4 chicken portions, on the bone

1 large onion, thinly sliced

400g/14oz can chopped tomatoes

150ml/¼ pint/⅔ cup red wine

1 garlic clove, crushed

1 rosemary sprig, finely chopped, plus extra whole sprigs to garnish

115g/4oz fresh field (portabello) mushrooms, thinly sliced

salt and ground black pepper

**1** Heat the oil and butter in a large, flameproof casserole until foaming. Add the chicken portions and fry for 5 minutes. Remove the chicken pieces and drain on kitchen paper.

**2** Add the sliced onion and cook gently, stirring frequently, for about 3 minutes then stir in the tomatoes and red wine.

**3** Add the crushed garlic and chopped rosemary and season. Bring to the boil, stirring continuously.

**4** Return the chicken to the casserole and turn to coat with the sauce. Cover with a tightly fitting lid and simmer gently for 30 minutes.

**5** Add the fresh mushrooms to the casserole and stir well to mix into the sauce. Continue simmering gently for 10 minutes, or until the chicken is tender. Taste and add more salt and ground black pepper if necessary. Garnish with the fresh rosemary sprigs. Serve hot, with creamy mashed potatoes or crusty white bread and butter, if you like.

**Per portion** Energy 386kcal/1622kJ; Protein 53.6g; Carbohydrate 4.5g, of which sugars 4.1g; Fat 14.5g, of which saturates 4.5g; Cholesterol 155mg; Calcium 28mg; Fibre 1.5g; Sodium 141mg.

# Braised farm pigeon with elderberry wine

Elderberry wine is made commercially by several companies in Scotland and is just one of many things that can be made from the tree. The berries are bitter on their own but make a deep, rich, almost port-like wine. Pigeons are best in the autumn.

**2** Brown the onion and then the mushrooms in the same pan, still over a medium heat, adding more oil if necessary. Add the vegetables to the casserole with the pigeon and mix around well.

**3** Pour in the stock, elderberry wine and just enough water to cover. Bring to the boil, cover tightly with a lid and cook in the preheated oven for 2 hours, until the pigeons are tender.

**4** Remove the birds from the casserole and keep warm. Boil the cooking liquor rapidly to thicken slightly. Return the pigeons to the pan and heat through. Serve with kale, if you like.

**Serves 4**

4 pigeons

15ml/1 tbsp plain (all-purpose) flour

30ml/2 tbsp olive oil, plus extra if needed

1 onion, chopped

225g/8oz button (white) mushrooms, sliced

250ml/8fl oz/1 cup dark stock

100ml/3½fl oz/scant ½ cup elderberry wine

salt and ground black pepper

kale, to serve (optional)

**1** Preheat the oven to 170°C/325°F/ Gas 3. Season the pigeons inside and out with salt and black pepper and roll liberally in the flour. Heat a heavy pan over a medium heat, add the olive oil and wait for it to bubble slightly. Brown the pigeons lightly all over, then transfer them to a casserole dish.

**Variation**

This recipe suits most game birds, so if you can't find pigeon, or it is the wrong season, you can use partridge, woodcock, pheasant or even wild duck or goose.

**Per portion** Energy 296kcal/1237kJ; Protein 31g; Carbohydrate 6.8g, of which sugars 2.5g; Fat 14.3g, of which saturates 0.1g; Cholesterol 0mg; Calcium 35mg; Fibre 1g; Sodium 117mg.

# Pheasant and wild mushroom ragoût

Although not indigenous to Scotland, pheasant has become so much a part of the autumnal landscape that it is hard to imagine them not there. With their proud strutting and red eye mascara they are stunning to look at, as well as making very good eating.

Serves 4

4 pheasant breasts, skinned

12 shallots, halved

2 garlic cloves, crushed

75g/3oz wild mushrooms, sliced

75ml/2½fl oz/⅓ cup port

150ml/¼ pint/⅔ cup chicken stock

sprigs of fresh parsley and thyme

1 bay leaf

grated rind of 1 lemon

200ml/7fl oz/scant 1 cup double (heavy) cream

salt and ground black pepper

**1** Dice and season the pheasant breasts. Heat a little oil in a heavy pan and colour the pheasant meat quickly. Remove from the pan and set aside.

**2** Add the shallots to the pan, fry quickly to colour a little then add the garlic and sliced mushrooms. Reduce the heat and cook gently for 5 minutes.

**3** Pour the port and stock into the pan and add the herbs and lemon rind. Reduce a little. When the shallots are nearly cooked add the cream, reduce to thicken then return the meat. Allow to cook for a few minutes before serving.

**Cook's Tip**
Serve with pilaff rice: fry a chopped onion, stir in 2.5cm/1in cinnamon stick, 2.5ml/½ tsp crushed cumin seeds, 2 crushed cardamom pods, a bay leaf and 5ml/1 tsp turmeric. Add 225g/8oz/ generous 1 cup long grain rice. Stir until well coated. Pour in 600ml/1 pint/2½ cups boiling water, cover then simmer gently for 15 minutes. Transfer to a serving dish, cover with a dish towel and leave for 5 minutes.

**Per portion** Energy 530kcal/2200kJ; Protein 34.1g; Carbohydrate 7.4g, of which sugars 5.9g; Fat 33g, of which saturates 20.2g; Cholesterol 69mg; Calcium 91mg; Fibre 1.1g; Sodium 114mg.

# Rabbit with apricots

Rabbit is a delicious meat, richer and more tasty than chicken, but with a similar colouring and texture. The gamey flavours go very well in many dishes, especially those with fruits and berries. Once a staple of the countryside, enjoyed by farmers and hunting parties alike, it is now available from good butchers and some fishmongers too.

**Serves 4**

2 rabbits

30ml/2 tbsp plain (all-purpose) flour

15ml/1 tbsp vegetable oil

90g/3½oz streaky (fatty) bacon, cut into thin pieces

10 baby (pearl) onions, peeled but kept whole

200ml/7fl oz/scant 1 cup dry white wine

1 bay leaf

12 dried apricots

salt and ground black pepper

**1** Ask your butcher to joint the rabbits, providing two legs and the saddle cut in two. Sprinkle the flour over a dish, season with salt and ground black pepper and mix well into the flour. Roll the rabbit pieces in it one by one to coat lightly all over, shaking off any excess flour. Set aside.

**2** Heat a heavy pan and add the oil. Brown the rabbit pieces all over then remove from the pan. Brown the bacon followed by the onions.

**3** Place the browned rabbit pieces, bacon and onions in a casserole. Pour the wine into the heavy pan and, over a low heat, scrape up all the bits from the base of the pan. Add a little water, bring to the boil and pour over the rabbit in the casserole, adding more water if needed to just cover.

**4** Add the bay leaf and bring to the boil. Allow to simmer gently for 40 minutes until the rabbit is tender.

**5** Remove the rabbit and onions from the pan and set aside, keeping them warm. Put the apricots into the pan and boil rapidly until the cooking liquor thickens slightly. Remove the bay leaf and check the seasoning. You can now either return the rabbit and onions to the pan as it is and heat before serving, or you can purée the apricots in the cooking liquor and pour the resulting rich sauce over the rabbit.

**Cook's Tip**
This dish is best reheated and served the next day so that the flavours can develop overnight.

Per portion Energy 481kcal/2022kJ; Protein 60.2g; Carbohydrate 22.5g, of which sugars 21.4g; Fat 13.8g, of which saturates 6.1g; Cholesterol 223mg; Calcium 153mg; Fibre 3.9g; Sodium 417mg.

# Roast hare with beetroot and crowdie

Hares are not the easiest of things to get hold of but in some parts of Scotland they are often available. This sauce goes well with venison too. Crowdie is a cream cheese made on every homestead up to the middle of the last century. For a less rich dish you could use plain yogurt in place of the crowdie at the end.

**Serves 4**

2 saddles of hare

10ml/2 tsp olive oil

350g/12oz cooked beetroot (beets)

30ml/2 tbsp chopped shallot

30ml/2 tbsp white wine vinegar

50g/2oz/¼ cup crowdie

5ml/1 tsp English mustard

salt and ground black pepper

**For the marinade**

600ml/1 pint/2½ cups red wine

1 carrot, finely diced

1 onion, finely diced

generous pinch of mixed herbs

pinch of salt

8 peppercorns

8 juniper berries

2 cloves

**1** Using a flexible knife, remove the membrane covering the saddles. Mix all the ingredients for the marinade together and coat the saddles then leave for one day, turning occasionally.

**2** Preheat the oven to 240°C/475°F/ Gas 9. Take out and dry the saddles with kitchen paper. Strain the marinade through a sieve and set aside.

**3** Heat the olive oil in a large ovenproof pan. Brown the saddles all over then cook in the preheated oven for 10– 15 minutes. They should still be pink. Leave in a warm place to rest.

**4** Remove most of the fat from the pan then add the beetroot. Cook for 1–2 minutes then add the shallot and cook for about 2 minutes to soften.

**5** Add the vinegar and 30ml/2 tbsp of the marinade and stir in thoroughly. Reduce the liquid until a coating texture is nearly achieved. Reduce the heat to low and add the crowdie. Whisk it in until completely melted, then add the mustard and season to taste. Set aside and keep warm.

**6** To serve, remove the fillets from the top and bottom of the saddles and slice lengthways. Place on four warmed plates and arrange the beetroot mixture on top. Reheat the sauce, without boiling, and hand round separately.

**Per portion** Energy 352kcal/1471kJ; Protein 41g; Carbohydrate 9.6g, of which sugars 8.7g; Fat 13.1g, of which saturates 6.5g; Cholesterol 136mg; Calcium 84mg; Fibre 1.9g; Sodium 255mg.

# Side dishes and accompaniments

Almost as tasty as the main course itself, the vegetables and salads in Scottish cuisine provide a healthy or hearty accompaniment to every meal. The richly flavoured green vegetables, including kale, chard, leeks and cabbage, are excellent served on their own or with a sauce. No meal is complete, however, without some robust vegetables, such as turnips, swedes or the versatile favourite, the potato.

# Clapshot

This root vegetable dish is excellent with haggis or on top of shepherd's pie in place of just potato. Turnips give an earthy flavour, and swede introduces a sweet accent. It is also slightly less heavy than mashed potato, which is ideal for a lighter meal or supper.

**Serves 4**

450g/1lb potatoes

450g/1lb turnips or swede (rutabaga)

50g/2oz/¼ cup butter

50ml/2fl oz/¼ cup milk

5ml/1 tsp freshly grated nutmeg

30ml/2 tbsp chopped fresh parsley

salt and ground black pepper

**1** Peel the potatoes and turnips or swede, then cut them into evenly sized small chunks. You will need a large sharp knife for the turnips.

**2** Place the chopped vegetables in a pan and cover with cold water. Bring to the boil over a medium heat, then reduce the heat and simmer until both vegetables are cooked, which will take about 15–20 minutes. Test the vegetables by pushing the point of a sharp knife into one of the cubes; if it goes in easily and the cube begins to break apart, then it is cooked.

**3** Drain the vegetables through a colander. Return to the pan and allow them to dry out for a few minutes over a low heat, stirring occasionally to prevent any from sticking to the base of the pan.

**4** Melt the butter with the milk in a small pan over a low heat. Mash the dry potato and turnip or swede mixture, then add the milk mixture. Grate in the nutmeg, add the parsley, mix thoroughly and season to taste. Serve immediately with roast meat or game.

**Per portion** Energy 204kcal/852kJ; Protein 3.4g; Carbohydrate 24.1g, of which sugars 7.2g; Fat 11.2g, of which saturates 6.8g; Cholesterol 27mg; Calcium 78mg; Fibre 3.8g; Sodium 111mg.

# Spiced greens

Here is a really tasty way to enliven your greens, excellent for crunchy cabbages but also good for kale and other purple sprouting leaves. Even Brussels sprout tops work well cooked like this. It's a very good way of persuading people to try leafy green vegetables.

**Serves 4**

1 medium cabbage, or the equivalent in quantity of your chosen green vegetable

15ml/1 tbsp groundnut (peanut) oil

5ml/1 tsp grated fresh root ginger

2 garlic cloves, grated

2 shallots, finely chopped

2 red chillies, seeded and finely sliced

salt and ground black pepper

**1** Remove any tough outer leaves from the cabbage then quarter it and remove the core. Shred the leaves.

**2** Pour the groundnut oil into a large pan and as it heats stir in the ginger and garlic. Add the shallots and as the pan becomes hotter add the chillies.

**3** Add the greens and toss to mix thoroughly. Cover the pan and reduce the heat to create some steam. Cook, shaking the pan occasionally, for about 3 minutes. Remove the lid and increase the heat to dry off the steam, season with salt and ground black pepper and serve immediately.

**Per portion** Energy 77kcal/322kJ; Protein 2.6g; Carbohydrate 9.9g, of which sugars 9.4g; Fat 3.1g, of which saturates 0.5g; Cholesterol 0mg; Calcium 90mg; Fibre 3.9g; Sodium 13mg.

# Spiced asparagus kale

Kale is a very important part of Scottish tradition. "Kailyards" was the word used to describe the kitchen garden, and even the midday meal was often referred to as "kail". Use the more widely available curly kale if you find it hard to get the asparagus variety.

**Serves 4**

175g/6oz asparagus kale

10ml/2 tsp butter

25g/1oz piece fresh root ginger, grated

15ml/1 tbsp soy sauce

salt and ground black pepper

**1** Prepare the kale by removing the centre stalk and ripping the leaves into smallish pieces.

**2** Heat a pan over a high heat and add the butter. As it melts, quickly add the kale and toss rapidly to allow the heat to cook it.

**3** Grate the ginger into the pan and stir in thoroughly. Then add the soy sauce and mix well. When the kale has wilted, it is ready to serve.

**Per portion** Energy 35kcal/145kJ; Protein 1.6g; Carbohydrate 0.9g, of which sugars 0.9g; Fat 2.8g, of which saturates 1.4g; Cholesterol 5mg; Calcium 58mg; Fibre 1.4g; Sodium 301mg.

# Braised red cabbage

Red cabbage is a hardy vegetable that can be grown in a garden plot even in the difficult conditions of the Highlands and Islands. Lightly spiced with a sharp, sweet flavour, braised red cabbage goes well with roast pork, duck and game dishes.

**Serves 4–6**

1kg/2¼lb red cabbage

2 cooking apples

2 onions, chopped

5ml/1 tsp freshly grated nutmeg

1.5ml/¼ tsp ground cloves

1.5ml/¼ tsp ground cinnamon

15ml/1 tbsp soft dark brown sugar

45ml/3 tbsp red wine vinegar

25g/1oz/2 tbsp butter, diced

salt and ground black pepper

chopped flat leaf parsley, to garnish

**1** Preheat the oven to 160°C/325°F/ Gas 3. Cut away and discard the large white ribs from the outer cabbage leaves using a large, sharp knife, then finely shred the cabbage. Peel, core and coarsely grate the apples.

**Cook's Tip**
This dish can be cooked in advance. Bake the cabbage for 1½ hours, then leave to cool. Store in a cool place covered with clear film (plastic wrap). To complete the cooking, bake it in the oven at 160°C/325°F/Gas 3 for about 30 minutes, stirring occasionally.

**2** Layer the shredded cabbage in a large ovenproof dish with the onions, apples, spices, sugar, and salt and ground black pepper. Pour over the vinegar and add the diced butter.

**3** Cover the dish with a lid and cook in the preheated oven for about 1½ hours, stirring a couple of times, until the cabbage is very tender. Serve immediately, garnished with the parsley.

**Per portion** Energy 160kcal/668kJ; Protein 4.3g; Carbohydrate 23.8g, of which sugars 22.4g; Fat 5.8g, of which saturates 3.3g; Cholesterol 13mg; Calcium 140mg; Fibre 6.6g; Sodium 58mg.

# Creamed leeks

This dish is a real Scottish favourite, delicious with a full roast dinner, or even on its own. It is very important to have good firm leeks without a core in the middle. The Scottish Musselburgh variety is excellent, if you can find it.

**Serves 4**

2 Musselburgh leeks, tops trimmed and roots removed

50g/2oz/½ stick butter

200ml/7fl oz/scant 1 cup double (heavy) cream

salt and ground black pepper

**Cook's Tip**

When buying leeks, choose smaller and less bendy ones as they are more tender.

**1** Split the leeks down the middle then cut across so you make pieces approximately 2cm/¾in square. Wash thoroughly and drain in a colander.

**2** Melt the butter in a large pan and when quite hot throw in the leeks, stirring to coat them in the butter, and heat through. They will wilt but should not exude water. Keep the heat high but don't allow them to colour. You need to create a balance between keeping the temperature high so the water steams out of the vegetable, keeping it bright green, whilst not burning the leeks.

**3** Keeping the heat high, pour in the cream, mix in thoroughly and allow to bubble and reduce. Season with salt and ground black pepper. When the texture is smooth, thick and creamy the leeks are ready to serve.

**Variation**

Although these leeks have a wonderful taste themselves, you may like to add extra flavourings, such as a little chopped garlic or some chopped fresh tarragon or thyme.

**Per portion** Energy 363kcal/1496kJ; Protein 2.5g; Carbohydrate 3.8g, of which sugars 3.1g; Fat 37.6g, of which saturates 23.3g; Cholesterol 95mg; Calcium 51mg; Fibre 2.2g; Sodium 89mg.

# Baked tomatoes with mint

This is a dish for the height of the summer when the tomatoes are falling off the vines and are very ripe, juicy and full of flavour. Mint flourishes in Lowland gardens and can also be nurtured in the Highlands. This tomato dish goes especially well with lamb.

**Serves 4**

6 large ripe tomatoes

300ml/½ pint/1¼ cups double (heavy) cream

2 sprigs of fresh mint

olive oil, for brushing

a few pinches of caster (superfine) sugar

30ml/2 tbsp grated Bonnet cheese

salt and ground black pepper

**1** Preheat the oven to 220°C/425°F/ Gas 7. Bring a pan of water to the boil and have a bowl of iced water ready. Cut the cores out of the tomatoes and make a cross at the base. Plunge the tomatoes into the boiling water for 10 seconds and then straight into the iced water. Leave to cool completely.

**2** Put the cream and mint in a pan and bring to the boil. Reduce the heat and allow to simmer until it has reduced by about half.

**3** Peel the cooled tomatoes and slice them thinly.

**Cook's Tip**
Bonnet is a hard goat's cheese but any hard, well-flavoured cheese will do.

**4** Brush a shallow gratin dish lightly with a little olive oil. Layer the sliced tomatoes in the dish, overlapping slightly, and season with salt and ground black pepper. Sprinkle a little sugar over the top.

**5** Strain the reduced cream evenly over the top of the tomatoes. Sprinkle on the cheese and bake in the preheated oven for 15 minutes, or until the top is browned and bubbling. Serve immediately in the gratin dish.

**Per portion** Energy 443kcal/1831kJ; Protein 5g; Carbohydrate 6.7g, of which sugars 6.7g; Fat 44.1g, of which saturates 27.4g; Cholesterol 113mg; Calcium 123mg; Fibre 1.8g; Sodium 105mg.

# Breads, bakes, preserves and sauces

Teatime in Scotland is the occasion for finding a wonderful spread of breads and sandwiches with jams and jellies. There is a great tradition of cake- and preserve-making, which have been part of the Scottish heritage for many years. Dried fruit and nuts are favourite ingredients for cakes, such as the famous moist Dundee cake, which has almonds baked decoratively around the top. Classic hedgerow and woodland berry jams and jellies are equally delicious and are made throughout the country.

# Scones with jam and cream

Scones, often known as biscuits in the US, are thought to originate from Scotland where they are still a popular part of afternoon tea with jams, jellies and thick clotted cream.

**Makes about 12**

450g/1lb/4 cups self-raising (self-rising) flour, or 450g/1lb/4 cups plain (all-purpose) flour and 10ml/2 tsp baking powder

5ml/1 tsp salt

50g/2oz/¼ cup butter, chilled and diced

15ml/1 tbsp lemon juice

about 400ml/14fl oz/1⅔ cups milk, plus extra to glaze

fruit jam and clotted cream or whipped double (heavy) cream, to serve

**1** Preheat the oven to 230°C/450°F/ Gas 8. Sift the flour, baking powder, if using, and salt into a clean, dry mixing bowl. Add the diced butter and rub it into the flour with your fingertips until the mixture resembles fine, evenly textured breadcrumbs.

**2** Whisk the lemon juice into the milk and leave for about 1 minute to thicken slightly, then pour into the flour mixture and mix quickly to form a soft but pliable dough. The wetter the mixture, the lighter the resulting scone will be, but if they are too wet they will spread during baking and lose their shape.

**3** Knead the dough lightly to form a ball, then roll it out on a floured surface to a thickness of at least 2.5cm/1in. Using a 5cm/2in pastry (cookie) cutter, and dipping it into flour each time, stamp out 12 scones. Place them on a well-floured baking sheet. Re-roll any trimmings and cut out more scones if you can.

**4** Brush the tops of the scones lightly with a little milk then bake in the preheated oven for about 20 minutes, or until risen and golden brown. Remove the baking sheet from the oven and wrap the scones in a clean dish towel to keep them warm and soft until ready to serve. Eat with your favourite fruit jam and a generous dollop of cream.

**Variation**
To make cheese scones, add 115g/4oz/1 cup of grated cheese (preferably Cheddar or another strong hard cheese) to the dough and knead it in thoroughly before rolling out.

**Per scone** Energy 170kcal/720kJ; Protein 4.5g; Carbohydrate 29.9g, of which sugars 2.1g; Fat 4.4g, of which saturates 2.6g; Cholesterol 11mg; Calcium 172mg; Fibre 1.2g; Sodium 338mg.

# Bere bannocks

Beremeal is a northern barley that grows well on Orkney, and you can still buy bannocks there made from it. Bannocks were traditionally made on a griddle but baking them in the oven works very well.

**Serves 6**

225g/8oz/2 cups beremeal flour

50g/2oz/½ cup plain
(all-purpose) flour

5ml/1 tsp cream of tartar

2.5ml/½ tsp salt

5ml/1 tsp bicarbonate of soda
(baking soda)

250ml/8fl oz/1 cup buttermilk or
natural (plain) yogurt

**1** Preheat the oven to 180°C/350°F/
Gas 4. Mix the beremeal flour, plain
flour, cream of tartar and salt together
in a bowl.

**2** Mix the bicarbonate of soda with the
buttermilk or yogurt then pour this
mixture into the dry ingredients.

**3** Mix the ingredients to form a soft
dough like a scone mix.

**Variation**
Bere bannocks are delicious if baked
with a little cheese on top. Use a harder
type of cheese, such as a good mature
cheddar or Bishop Kennedy, and grate
about 50g/2oz/½ cup over the surface
before you put it into the oven to bake.
The result is very tasty hot or cold for
breakfast or lunch.

**4** Turn the dough out on to a floured
surface and press down with your
hands to make the whole dough
about 1cm/½in thick.

**5** Cut the dough into six segments and
place on an oiled baking sheet. Bake in
the oven for about 15 minutes, or until
lightly browned.

**Per bannock** Energy 280kcal/1192kJ; Protein 8.8g; Carbohydrate 61.4g, of which sugars 4.9g; Fat 1.8g, of which saturates 0.4g; Cholesterol 1mg; Calcium 148mg; Fibre 0.4g; Sodium 54mg.

# Black bun

This is a very traditional Scottish sweetmeat, eaten with a nip or two of whisky at the Hogmanay New Year festivities, and often given to visitors on New Year's Day. It is different from most fruit cakes because it is baked in a pastry case. It should be made several weeks in advance to give it time to mature properly.

**Makes 1 cake**

**For the pastry**

225g/8oz/2 cups plain (all-purpose) flour

115g/4oz/½ cup butter

5ml/1 tsp baking powder

cold water

**For the filling**

500g/1¼lb/4 cups raisins

675g/1½lb/3 cups currants

115g/4oz/1 cup chopped almonds

175g/6oz/1½ cups plain (all-purpose) flour

115g/4oz/generous ½ cup soft light brown sugar

5ml/1 tsp ground allspice

2.5ml/½ tsp each ground ginger, ground cinnamon and ground black pepper

2.5ml/½ tsp baking powder

5ml/1 tsp cream of tartar

15ml/1 tbsp brandy

1 egg, beaten, plus extra for glazing

about 75ml/5 tbsp milk

**1** First make the pastry. Sift the plain flour into a mixing bowl. Remove the butter from the refrigerator ahead of time and dice it into small cubes. Leave it out of the refrigerator to soften well.

**2** Add the cubes of butter to the flour. Rub the butter into the flour with your fingertips until it is the consistency of breadcrumbs. Add the baking powder and mix well. Then add small amounts of cold water, blending it in with a fork, until you can handle the mixture and knead it into a stiff dough.

**3** On a floured surface, roll out the dough to a thin sheet. Grease a 20cm/8in loaf tin (pan) and line with the thin sheet of dough. Leave enough to cover the top of the cake.

**4** Preheat the oven to 110°C/225°F/ Gas ¼. For the filling, put all the dry ingredients together in a dry warm bowl, including the ground spices and cream of tartar. Mix them together with a spoon until they are thoroughly blended.

**5** Stir the brandy and egg into the dry filling mixture and add enough milk to moisten the mixture.

**6** Put the filling into the prepared tin and cover with the remaining pastry.

**7** Prick all over with a fork and brush with egg. Bake in the preheated oven for about 3 hours. Remove from the oven and leave to cool on a wire rack. Store in an airtight container.

**Per cake** Energy 1752kcal/7403kJ; Protein 25.8g; Carbohydrate 323.7g, of which sugars 241.9g; Fat 47.4g, of which saturates 18.5g; Cholesterol 115mg; Calcium 496mg; Fibre 11.4g; Sodium 324mg.

# Shortbread

The quintessential Scottish snack, shortbread is a great speciality and favourite with the Scots. It is wonderfully satisfying at any time of the day or night.

**Makes about 48 fingers**

oil, for greasing

275g/10oz/2½ cups plain (all-purpose) flour

25g/1oz/¼ cup ground almonds

225g/8oz/1 cup butter, softened

75g/3oz/scant ½ cup caster (superfine) sugar

grated rind of ½ lemon

**1** Preheat the oven to 180°C/350°F/ Gas 4 and oil a large Swiss roll tin (jelly roll pan) or baking tray.

**2** Put the remaining ingredients into a blender or food processor and pulse until the mixture comes together.

**3** Place the mixture on the oiled tray and flatten it out with a palette knife or metal spatula until evenly spread. Bake in the preheated oven for 20 minutes, or until pale golden brown.

**Variation**
You can replace the lemon rind with the grated rind of two oranges for a tangy orange flavour, if you prefer.

**4** Remove from the oven and immediately mark the shortbread into fingers or squares while the mixture is soft. Allow to cool a little, and then transfer to a wire rack and leave until cold. If stored in an airtight container, the shortbread should keep for up to two weeks.

**Cook's Tip**
To make by hand, sift the flour and almonds on to a pastry board or work surface. Cream together the butter and sugar in a mixing bowl and then turn the creamed mixture on to the pastry board with the flour and almonds. Work the mixture together using your fingertips. It should come together to make a smooth dough. Continue as above from Step 3.

**Per finger** Energy 64kcal/266kJ; Protein 0.7g; Carbohydrate 6.1g, of which sugars 1.8g; Fat 4.2g, of which saturates 2.5g; Cholesterol 10mg; Calcium 11mg; Fibre 0.2g; Sodium 29mg.

# Dundee cake

A classic Scottish fruit cake, this is made with mixed peel, dried fruit, almonds and spices. It is decorated in the traditional way, covered completely with whole blanched almonds.

**Serves 16–20**

175g/6oz/¾ cup butter

175g/6oz/¾ cup soft light brown sugar

3 eggs

225g/8oz/2 cups plain (all-purpose) flour

10ml/2 tsp baking powder

5ml/1 tsp ground cinnamon

2.5ml/½ tsp ground cloves

1.5ml/¼ tsp freshly grated nutmeg

225g/8oz/generous 1½ cups sultanas (golden raisins)

175g/6oz/¾ cup glacé (candied) cherries

115g/4oz/⅔ cup mixed chopped (candied) peel

50g/2oz/½ cup blanched almonds, roughly chopped

grated rind of 1 lemon

30ml/2 tbsp brandy

75g/3oz/¾ cup whole blanched almonds, to decorate

**1** Preheat the oven to 160°C/325°F/ Gas 3. Grease and line a 20cm/8in round, deep cake tin (pan).

**2** Cream the butter and sugar together in a large mixing bowl. Add the eggs, one at a time, beating thoroughly after each addition.

**Cook's Tip**
All rich fruit cakes improve in flavour if left in a cool place for up to 3 months. Wrap the cake in baking parchment and a double layer of foil.

**3** Sift the flour, baking powder and spices together. Fold into the creamed mixture alternately with the remaining ingredients, apart from the whole almonds. Mix until evenly blended. Transfer the mixture to the prepared tin and smooth the surface, making a dip in the centre.

**4** Decorate the top by pressing the almonds in decreasing circles over the entire surface. Bake in the preheated oven for 2–2¼ hours, until a skewer inserted in the centre comes out clean.

**5** Cool in the tin for 30 minutes then transfer to a wire rack to cool fully.

**Per portion** Energy 321kcal/1347kJ; Protein 4.7g; Carbohydrate 44.2g, of which sugars 33.3g; Fat 14.7g, of which saturates 6.4g; Cholesterol 59mg; Calcium 76mg; Fibre 1.7g; Sodium 107mg.

# Raspberry jam

For many this is the best of all jams: it is delicious with scones and cream. Raspberries are low in pectin and acid, so they will not set firmly – but a soft set is perfect for this jam. Enjoy it lavishly smothered on scones or toasted tealoaf.

**Makes about 3.1kg/7lb**

1.8kg/4lb/10⅔ cups firm raspberries

juice of 1 large lemon

1.8kg/4lb/9 cups sugar, warmed

**Cook's Tip**
To test if jam or jelly will set, put a spoonful of jam or jelly on to a cold saucer. Allow it to cool slightly and then push the surface of the jam with your finger. Setting point has been reached if a skin has formed and it wrinkles. If not, boil for a little longer and keep testing regularly until it sets; the flavour will be better if the boiling time is short.

**1** Put 175g/6oz/1 cup of the raspberries into a preserving pan and crush them. Add the rest of the fruit and the lemon juice, and simmer until soft and pulpy. Add the sugar and stir until dissolved, then bring back to the boil and boil hard until setting point is reached, testing after 3–4 minutes.

**2** Pour into warmed, sterilized jars. When cold, cover, seal and store in a cool, dark place for up to 6 months.

**Variation**
For a slightly stronger flavour, 150ml/ ¼ pint/⅔ cup redcurrant juice can be used instead of the lemon juice.

**Per batch** Energy 7542kcal/32,220kJ; Protein 34.2g; Carbohydrate 1963.8g, of which sugars 1963.8g; Fat 5.4g, of which saturates 1.8g; Cholesterol 0mg; Calcium 1.40g; Fibre 45g; Sodium 162mg

# Whisky marmalade

Real home-made marmalade tastes delicious, and flavouring it with whisky makes it a special treat. This is an adaptation of the commercial method, in which marmalade is matured in old whisky barrels and takes the flavour from the wood.

**Makes 3.6–4.5kg/8–10lb**

1.3kg/3lb Seville (Temple) oranges

juice of 2 large lemons

2.75kg/6lb/13½ cups
sugar, warmed

about 300ml/½ pint/1¼ cups whisky

**1** Scrub the oranges thoroughly using a nylon brush and pick off the disc at the stalk end. Cut the oranges in half widthways and squeeze the juice, retaining the pips (seeds). Quarter the peel, cut away and reserve any thick white pith, and shred the peel – thickly or thinly depending on how you prefer the finished marmalade.

**2** Cut up the reserved pith roughly and tie it up with the pips in a square of muslin (cheesecloth) using a long piece of string. Tie the bag loosely, so that water can circulate during cooking and will extract the pectin from the pith and pips. Hang the bag from the handle of the preserving pan.

**3** Add the cut peel, strained juices and 3.5 litres/6 pints/15 cups water to the pan. Bring to the boil and simmer for 1½–2 hours, or until the peel is very tender (it will not soften further once the sugar has been added).

**4** Lift up the bag of pith and pips and squeeze it out well between two plates over the pan to extract as much of the juices as possible as these contain valuable pectin. Add the sugar to the pan and stir over a low heat until it has completely dissolved.

**5** Bring to the boil and boil hard for 15–20 minutes or until setting point is reached. To test, allow a spoon of the mixture to cool slightly, and then push the surface to see if a skin has formed. If not, boil a little longer.

**6** Skim, if necessary, and leave to cool for about 15 minutes, then stir to redistribute the peel. Divide the whisky among 8–10 warmed, sterilized jars and swill it around. Using a small heatproof jug (pitcher), pour in the marmalade.

**7** Cover and seal while still hot. Label when cold, and store in a cool, dark place for up to 6 months.

**Per batch** Energy 10,736kcal/45,734kJ; Protein 22.8g; Carbohydrate 2657.8g, of which sugars 2657.8g; Fat 1.3g, of which saturates 0g; Cholesterol 0mg; Calcium 1.74g; Fibre 15.6g; Sodium 187mg.

# Garden jam

Soft fruit is widely grown in Scottish gardens and, after the first flush of early fruit is over, much of it is used for preserves, such as this useful mixed fruit jam.

**Makes about 3.6kg/8lb**

450g/1lb/4 cups blackcurrants
(stalks removed)

450g/1lb/4 cups blackberries
(or whitecurrants or redcurrants)

450g/1lb/2²⁄₃ cups raspberries
(or loganberries)

450g/1lb/4 cups strawberries

1.8kg/4lb/9 cups granulated
sugar, warmed

**Cook's Tip**
To reduce the risk of mould forming, cover and seal preserves while they are either very hot or when absolutely cold as this prevents condensation.

**1** Put the blackcurrants into a large preserving pan and add 150ml/¹⁄₄ pint/ ²⁄₃ cup water. Bring to the boil and simmer until the berries are almost cooked. Add the rest of the fruit and simmer gently, stirring occasionally, for about 10 minutes, or until the fruit is just turning soft.

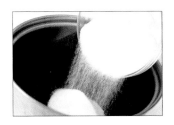

**2** Add the warm sugar to the pan and stir over a gentle heat until it is completely dissolved.

**3** Bring to the boil and boil hard until setting point is reached. To test, put a spoonful of jam on to a cold saucer. Cool slightly, then push the surface. It is ready if a skin has formed and it wrinkles to the touch. If not, boil for longer and keep testing until it sets.

**4** Remove any scum from the jam and pour into sterilized, warm jars. Cover and seal. Store in a cool, dark place for up to 6 months.

Per batch Energy 7583kcal/32,328kJ; Protein 23.9g; Carbohydrate 1991.7g, of which sugars 1991.7g; Fat 1.4g, of which saturates 0g; Cholesterol 0mg; Calcium 1.44g; Fibre 31.1g; Sodium 203mg.

# Rowan jelly

This astringent jelly is made from the orange fruit of mountain ash trees, which flourish in areas where deer run wild. It is a traditional accompaniment to game, especially venison.

**Makes about 2.25kg/5lb**

1.3kg/3lb/12 cups rowanberries

450g/1lb crab apples, or windfall cooking apples

450g/1lb/2¼ cups granulated sugar per 600ml/1 pint/2½ cups juice, warmed

**1** Cut the rowanberries off their stalks, rinse them in a colander and put them into a preserving pan.

**2** Remove any badly damaged parts from the apples before weighing them, then cut them up roughly without peeling or coring them. Add the apples to the pan, with 1.2 litres/2 pints/ 5 cups water, which should just about cover the fruit.

**3** Bring to the boil and simmer for about 45 minutes, until the fruit is soft, stirring occasionally and crushing the fruit with a wooden spoon to help extract the pectin. Strain the fruit through a jelly bag or fine sieve into a bowl overnight. Discard the fruit.

**4** Measure the juice and allow 450g/1lb/2¼ cups sugar per 600ml/ 1 pint/2½ cups juice. Return the juice to the rinsed preserving pan and add the measured amount of sugar. Stir the mixture thoroughly.

**5** Stir over a low heat until the sugar has dissolved, and then bring to the boil and boil hard for about 10 minutes until setting point is reached. To test, put a spoonful of jam on to a cold saucer. Allow to cool slightly, and then push the surface with your finger to see if a skin has formed. If not, boil longer.

**6** Skim, if necessary, and pour into warmed, sterilized jars. Cover, seal and store in a cool, dark place until needed. The jelly will store well for 6 months.

**Variations**
• The thinly peeled rind and juice of a lemon can be included for a firmer set; reduce the amount of water slightly to allow for the lemon juice.
• For sloe jelly, substitute 1.3kg/3lb sloes (black plums) for the rowan berries and use 675g/1½lb apples.

**Cook's Tip**
For a less astringent jelly, an equal quantity of apples and berries may be used, such as 900g/2lb of each.

**Per batch** Energy 2340kcal/9993kJ; Protein 15.8g; Carbohydrate 606.4g, of which sugars 606.4g; Fat 0.5g, of which saturates 0g; Cholesterol 0mg; Calcium 1.03g; Fibre 54g; Sodium 80mg.

# Tomato chutney

This spicy and dark, sweet-sour chutney is delicious served with a selection of well-flavoured cheeses and crackers, oatcakes or bread. It is also popular in sandwiches and chunky lunchtime rolls packed with cold roast meats such as ham, turkey, tongue or lamb. Use it also as a condiment or table sauce for meats.

**Makes about 1.8kg/4lb**

900g/2lb tomatoes, skinned

225g/8oz/1½ cups raisins

225g/8oz onions, chopped

225g/8oz/generous 1 cup caster (superfine) sugar

600ml/1 pint/2½ cups malt vinegar

**Variations**
• Dried dates may be used in place of the raisins. Stone (pit) and chop them into small pieces. You can also buy stoned cooking dates that have been compressed in a block and these will need chopping finely.
• Red wine vinegar or sherry vinegar may be used in place of the malt vinegar, making a more delicate flavour.

**1** Chop the tomatoes roughly and place in a preserving pan. Add the raisins, onions and caster sugar.

**2** Pour the vinegar into the pan and bring the mixture to the boil over a medium heat. Reduce the heat and simmer for 2 hours, uncovered, until soft and thickened.

**3** Transfer the chutney to warmed sterilized jars. Top with waxed discs to prevent moulds from growing. Use good airtight lids, especially if you mean to store for a long period. Store in a cool, dark place and leave to mature for at least 1 month before use.

**Cook's Tip**
The chutney will keep unopened for up to 1 year if properly airtight and stored in a cool place. Once the jars have been opened, store in the refrigerator and use within 1 month.

**Per batch** Energy 1733kcal/7385kJ; Protein 14.9g; Carbohydrate 436.7g, of which sugars 431.6g; Fat 4.1g, of which saturates 0.9g; Cholesterol 0mg; Calcium 342mg; Fibre 16.6g; Sodium 236mg.

# Mushroom sauce

This sauce is ideal as an addition to soups and stews and can be added to meat and game sauces for an extra boost of woodland flavour. You can use either wild or cultivated mushrooms for this recipe. Traditionally it would have been made in large quantities when the wild mushrooms were available, and then stored.

**Makes 150ml/¼ pint/¾ cup**

mushrooms and salt (see Step 1)

**For the spice mix**

3 garlic cloves, chopped

2 red chillies, seeded and chopped

5ml/1 tsp ground allspice

2.5ml/½ tsp freshly grated nutmeg

2.5ml/½ tsp ground ginger

300ml/½ pint/1¼ cups red wine

**1** You will need 15ml/1 tbsp salt for every 450g/1lb mushrooms used. Roughly chop the mushrooms and place in a large ovenproof pan, sprinkling the salt on as you go.

**2** Leave, covered in clear film (plastic wrap), for 3 days to exude the juices, giving them a press occasionally.

**3** Preheat the oven to 110°C/225°F/ Gas 2. Heat the pan of mushrooms in the oven for 3 hours to get the last of the moisture out.

**Cook's Tip**
The sauce will keep for a few months unopened. Once opened keep in the refrigerator and use within 1 month.

**4** Strain the mushrooms. Measure the quantity of strained mushroom liquid: for every 1 litre/1¾ pints/4 cups of liquid, allow one batch of the spice mix listed in the ingredients including the wine.

**5** Add the spices and wine to the mushroom liquid and bring to the boil. Return to the oven for 2–3 hours. Strain the sauce and pour into warmed sterilized jars or bottles. Use as required to flavour sauces and stews.

Per batch Energy 321kcal/1344kJ; Protein 16.5g; Carbohydrate 4.2g, of which sugars 2.4g; Fat 4.5g, of which saturates 0.9g; Cholesterol 0mg; Calcium 75mg; Fibre 9.9g; Sodium 66mg.

# Desserts
# and drinks

Not only are the Scots well known for their sweet tooth, they are also famous for their whisky. Each clan's whisky had a unique flavour, its quality a sign of the clan's prestige and power. Today, whisky is produced in a number of distilleries around the country. The Scots also enjoy some scrumptious desserts. A recurring theme is fresh berries – especially raspberries – baked in tarts, crumbles and pies or blended with creams and other dairy products. These tasty morsels are available to all to pick wild from the woodlands and hedgerows.

# Cranachan

This lovely, nutritious dish is based on a traditional Scottish recipe originally made to celebrate the Harvest Festival. It can be enjoyed, as the original recipe was, as a teatime treat or a dessert, but it is also excellent served for breakfast or brunch. Try fresh blueberries or blackberries in place of the raspberries, too.

**Serves 4**

75g/3oz crunchy oat cereal

600ml/1 pint/2½ cups Greek (US strained plain) yogurt

250g/9oz/1⅓ cups raspberries

heather honey, to serve

**1** Preheat the grill (broiler) to high. Spread the oat cereal on a baking sheet and place under the hot grill for 3–4 minutes, stirring regularly. Set aside on a plate to cool.

**2** When the cereal has cooled completely, fold it into the Greek yogurt, then gently fold in 200g/7oz/generous 1 cup of the raspberries, being careful not to crush them.

**3** Spoon the yogurt mixture into four serving glasses or dishes, top with the remaining raspberries and serve immediately. Pass around a dish of heather honey to drizzle over the top for extra sweetness and flavour.

**Variations**
• You can use almost any berries for this recipe. Strawberries and blackberries work very well. If you use strawberries, remove the stalks and cut them into quarters beforehand.
• If you feel especially decadent, you can use clotted cream instead of yogurt.

**Per portion** Energy 276kcal/1152kJ; Protein 12.4g; Carbohydrate 17.2g, of which sugars 11.1g; Fat 19.7g, of which saturates 8.7g; Cholesterol 0mg; Calcium 255mg; Fibre 2.5g; Sodium 122mg.

# Strawberry cream shortbreads

These attractive and appetizing treats are always popular, especially served with afternoon tea or as a quick and easy dessert. Serve them as soon as they are ready because the shortbread cookies will lose their lovely crisp texture if left to stand for a long time.

**Serves 3**

150g/5oz/1¼ cups strawberries

450ml/¾ pint/scant 2 cups double (heavy) cream

6 round shortbread biscuits (cookies)

**1** Reserve three attractive strawberries for decoration. Hull the remaining strawberries and cut them in half, discarding any bad parts.

**2** Put the halved strawberries in a bowl and gently crush them using the back of a fork. Only crush the berries lightly; they should not be reduced to a purée. A few larger chunks should still be left whole to add to the texture.

**3** Put the cream in a large, clean bowl and whip until softly peaking. Add the crushed strawberries and gently fold in to combine. (Do not overmix.)

**4** Halve the reserved strawberries – you can choose whether to leave the stalks intact or to remove them.

**5** Spoon the strawberry and cream mixture on top of the shortbread cookies. Decorate each one with half a strawberry and serve immediately.

**Variations**
• You can use any other berry you like for this dessert – try raspberries or blueberries.
• Two ripe, peeled peaches will also give great results.
• Instead of shortbread, you can use freshly baked scones.

Per portion Energy 976kcal/4035kJ; Protein 5.7g; Carbohydrate 34.6g, of which sugars 16.8g; Fat 90.8g, of which saturates 50.1g; Cholesterol 206mg; Calcium 122mg; Fibre 1.3g; Sodium 204mg.

# Rhubarb fool

Here is a quick and simple dessert that makes the most of field-grown rhubarb when it is in season. Serve with Scottish shortbread and pass around a dish of heather honey for those with a sweet tooth.

**1** Cut the rhubarb into pieces and wash thoroughly. Stew over a low heat with just the water clinging to it and the sugar. This takes about 10 minutes. Set aside to cool.

**2** Pass the rhubarb through a fine sieve so you have a thick purée.

**3** Use equal parts of the purée, the whipped double cream and thick custard. Combine the purée and custard first then fold in the cream.

**4** Chill in the refrigerator before serving. Serve with heather honey.

**Serves 4**

450g/1lb rhubarb, trimmed

75g/3oz/scant ½ cup soft light brown sugar

whipped double (heavy) cream and ready-made thick custard (see Step 3)

**Variations**
• You can use another fruit if you like for this dessert – try bramble fruits or apples. Other stewed fruits also work well, such as prunes or peaches. For something a little more exotic, you can use mangoes.
• For a low-fat option, substitute natural (plain) yogurt for the cream.

**Per portion** Energy 439kcal/1828kJ; Protein 4.6g; Carbohydrate 34.1g, of which sugars 31.8g; Fat 31.7g, of which saturates 18.9g; Cholesterol 80mg; Calcium 233mg; Fibre 1.6g; Sodium 74mg.

# Border tart

The Borders are particularly associated with sweet tarts that make tasty mid-morning snacks, as well as satisfying desserts. This one is delicious served hot or cold with cream.

**Serves 4**

250g/9oz sweet pastry (see Auld Alliance Apple Tart)

1 egg

75g/3oz/scant ½ cup soft light brown sugar

50g/2oz/¼ cup butter, melted

10ml/2 tsp white wine vinegar

115g/4oz/½ cup currants

25g/1oz/¼ cup chopped walnuts

double (heavy) cream, to serve (optional)

**1** Line a 20cm/8in flan tin (tart pan) with sweet pastry. Preheat the oven to 190°C/375°F/Gas 5. Mix the egg, sugar and melted butter together.

**2** Stir the vinegar, currants and walnuts into the egg mixture.

**3** Pour the mixture into the pastry case and bake in the preheated oven for 30 minutes. Remove from the oven when thoroughly cooked, take out of the flan tin and leave to cool on a wire rack for at least 30 minutes. Serve on its own or with a dollop of fresh cream.

**Per portion** Energy 312kcal/1307kJ; Protein 3.4g; Carbohydrate 41.1g, of which sugars 41g; Fat 16.1g, of which saturates 7.3g; Cholesterol 74mg; Calcium 54mg; Fibre 0.8g; Sodium 99mg.

# Raspberry and almond tart

Raspberries grow best in a cool, damp climate, making them a natural choice for Scottish gardeners. Juicy ripe raspberries and almonds go very well together. This is a rich tart, ideal for serving at the end of a special lunch or at a dinner party.

**Serves 4**

200g/7oz sweet pastry (see Auld Alliance Apple Tart)

2 large (US extra large) eggs

75ml/2½fl oz/⅓ cup double (heavy) cream

50g/2oz/¼ cup caster (superfine) sugar

50g/2oz/½ cup ground almonds

20g/¾oz/4 tsp butter

350g/12oz/2 cups raspberries

**1** Line a 20cm/8in flan tin (tart pan) with the pastry. Prick the base all over and leave to rest for at least 30 minutes. Preheat the oven to 200°C/400°F/Gas 6.

**2** Put the eggs, cream, sugar and ground almonds in a bowl and whisk together briskly. Melt the butter and pour into the mixture, stirring to combine thoroughly.

**3** Sprinkle the raspberries evenly over the pastry case. The ones at the top will appear through the surface, so keep them evenly spaced. You can also create a pattern with them.

**4** Pour the egg and almond mixture over the top. Once again ensure that it is spread evenly throughout the tart.

**5** Bake in the preheated oven for 25 minutes. Serve warm or cold.

**Variation**

Peaches make a very attractive and tasty tart. Use 6 large, ripe peaches and remove the skin and stone (pit). Cut into slices and use in the same way as the raspberries above.

Per portion Energy 548kcal/2284kJ; Protein 10.9g; Carbohydrate 41.7g, of which sugars 18.4g; Fat 38.8g, of which saturates 14.8g; Cholesterol 158mg; Calcium 128mg; Fibre 4.1g; Sodium 282mg.

# Auld Alliance apple tart

The Auld Alliance is a friendship that has existed between France and Scotland for some 600 years and as well as sharing friendship the two countries have also shared ideas on food. This is a classic French pudding that has been adapted by the Scots.

**Serves 4**

200g/7oz/1 cup butter

200g/7oz/1 cup caster (superfine) sugar

6 large eating apples

**For the sweet pastry**

150g/5oz/10 tbsp butter

50g/2oz/¼ cup caster (superfine) sugar

225g/8oz/2 cups plain (all-purpose) flour

1 egg

**1** Make the sweet pastry. Cream the butter with the caster sugar together in a food processor. Add the plain flour and egg. Mix until just combined, being careful not to overprocess. Leave in a cool place for an hour before use.

**2** Preheat the oven to 200°C/400°F/ Gas 6. Make the filling. Cut the butter into small pieces. Using a shallow, 30cm/12in ovenproof frying pan, heat the sugar and butter and allow to caramelize over a low heat, stirring gently continuously. This will take about 10 minutes.

**3** Meanwhile peel and core the apples then cut them into eighths. When the butter and sugar are caramelized, place the apples in the pan in a circular fan, one layer around the outside then one in the centre. The pan should be full. Reduce the heat and cook the apples for 5 minutes then remove from heat.

**4** Roll out the pastry to a circle big enough to fit the pan completely with generous edgings.

**5** Spread the pastry over the fruit and tuck in the edges. Bake in the oven for about 30 minutes, or until the pastry is browned and set.

**6** When cooked remove the tart from the oven and leave to rest. When ready to serve, gently reheat on the stove for a few minutes then invert on to a warmed serving plate, with the pastry on the base and the apples caramelized on the top.

**Per portion** Energy 904kcal/3774kJ; Protein 4.6g; Carbohydrate 95.2g, of which sugars 66.5g; Fat 58.8g, of which saturates 31.5g; Cholesterol 116mg; Calcium 95mg; Fibre 3.6g; Sodium 559mg.

# Scone and fresh fruit pudding

This luscious dessert incorporates good Scottish ingredients – sweet, juicy strawberries and raspberries in season, cream crowdie (a curd cheese) and a scone topping. Served with fresh cream or custard, it is perfect to finish a dinner party or hearty Sunday lunch.

**3** Dot spoonfuls of the crowdie over the fruit. If you can't get crowdie, use a good thick Greek (US strained plain) yogurt instead.

**Serves 4**

450g/1lb/4 cups strawberries

250g/9oz/1½ cups raspberries

50g/2oz/¼ cup soft light brown sugar

**For the scone topping**

175g/6oz/1½ cups self-raising (self-rising) flour

5ml/1 tsp baking powder

50g/2oz/¼ cup soft light brown sugar

grated rind of 1 lemon

50g/2oz/¼ cup butter, melted

1 egg, beaten

250g/9oz cream crowdie

**1** Preheat the oven to 220°C/425°F/ Gas 7. Gently mix the fruit with the sugar then place in a bowl in an ovenproof dish.

**2** For the scone topping, combine the flour, baking powder and sugar in a bowl with the grated lemon rind then add the melted butter and beaten egg and mix thoroughly.

**4** Place a scoop of the scone dough on top of each spoon of crowdie. Bake for about 20 minutes. The crowdie or yogurt should be oozing out of the scone topping. Serve immediately, and pass around a dish of crowdie (or yogurt) for those who want more.

**Variations**
• Many other fruits can be used for this wonderful and easy dessert. If you prefer, try orchard fruits such as apples, pears, apricots and peaches. Plums work particularly well, and the flavour can be enhanced with the juice of an orange or lemon.
• If you prefer, you can prepare the recipe without the crowdie (or yogurt) baked into the pie. Serve it on the side, or use custard or thick cream instead.

**Per portion** Energy 474kcal/1996kJ; Protein 11.6g; Carbohydrate 70.2g, of which sugars 37.7g; Fat 19g, of which saturates 10.4g; Cholesterol 79mg; Calcium 304mg; Fibre 4.2g; Sodium 307mg.

# Plum crumble

The crumble is a perennially popular dessert. Plums can be divided into three categories – dessert, dual and cooking. Choose whichever dual or cooking plum is available locally, although Victoria plums would commonly be used in Scotland.

**Serves 4**

450g/1lb stoned (pitted) plums

50g/2oz/¼ cup soft light brown sugar

15ml/1 tbsp water

juice of 1 lemon

**For the crumble topping**

50g/2oz/½ cup plain (all-purpose) flour

25g/1oz/generous ¼ cup coarse rolled oats

50g/2oz/¼ cup soft light brown sugar

50g/2oz/¼ cup butter, softened

**1** Preheat the oven to 200°C/400°F/ Gas 6. Place a large pan over a medium heat. Put the plums in the pan and add the sugar, water and lemon juice. Mix thoroughly and bring to the boil, stirring continuously until the sugar dissolves. Cook the plums until they are just beginning to soften. Place the fruit with the juices in a deep pie dish.

**2** Place the crumble ingredients in a bowl and mix with your fingers until the mixture resembles breadcrumbs.

**3** Sprinkle the crumble topping evenly over the fruit so that it is a good thickness. Bake in the preheated oven for 20 minutes, or until the top is crunchy and brown.

**Per portion** Energy 304kcal/1284kJ; Protein 2.9g; Carbohydrate 51.5g, of which sugars 37.4g; Fat 11.1g, of which saturates 6.5g; Cholesterol 27mg; Calcium 53mg; Fibre 2.8g; Sodium 82mg.

# Malt whisky truffles

Malt whisky has long been used to flavour Scottish dishes. Here is a new speciality, blending rich chocolate with cool cream and potent whisky for a mouthwatering end to any meal.

**Makes 25–30**

200g/7oz dark (bittersweet) chocolate, chopped into small pieces

150ml/¼ pint/⅔ cup double (heavy) cream

45ml/3 tbsp malt whisky

115g/4oz/1 cup icing (confectioners') sugar

cocoa powder, for coating

**1** Melt the chocolate in a heatproof bowl over a pan of simmering water, stirring continuously until smooth. Allow to cool slightly.

**2** Using a wire whisk, whip the cream with the whisky in a bowl until thick enough to hold its shape.

**Variation**
You can also make Drambuie truffles by using Drambuie instead of whisky.

**3** Stir in the melted chocolate and icing sugar and leave until firm enough to handle. Dust your hands with cocoa powder and shape the mixture into bite-sized balls. Coat in cocoa powder and pack into pretty cases or boxes. Store in the refrigerator for 3–4 days.

**Per portion** Energy 93kcal/387kJ; Protein 0.5g; Carbohydrate 10g, of which sugars 9.9g; Fat 5.5g, of which saturates 3.3g; Cholesterol 9mg; Calcium 8mg; Fibre 0.2g; Sodium 2mg.

# Whisky mac cream

The warming tipple whisky mac is a combination of whisky and ginger wine. This recipe turns the drink into a rich, smooth, creamy dessert – very decadent.

**Serves 4**

4 egg yolks

15ml/1 tbsp caster (superfine) sugar, plus 50g/2oz/¼ cup

600ml/1 pint/2½ cups double (heavy) cream

15ml/1 tbsp whisky

green ginger wine, to serve

**1** Whisk the egg yolks thoroughly with the first, smaller amount of caster sugar. Whisk briskly until they are light and pale.

**2** Pour the cream into a pan with the whisky and the rest of the caster sugar. Bring to scalding point but do not boil, then pour on to the egg yolks, whisking continually. Return to the pan and, over a low heat, stir until the custard thickens slightly.

**3** Pour into individual ramekin dishes, cover each with clear film (plastic wrap) and leave overnight to set.

**4** To serve, pour just enough green ginger wine over the top of each ramekin to cover the cream.

Per portion Energy 892kcal/3682kJ; Protein 5.4g; Carbohydrate 19.7g, of which sugars 19.7g; Fat 86.1g, of which saturates 51.7g; Cholesterol 407mg; Calcium 107mg; Fibre 0g; Sodium 44mg.

# Sparkling elderflower drink

The elder tree not only produces berries for wine but the fragrant flowers have a very pungent aroma and flavour. Unfortunately the elderflower season is short, just before the berries appear, so take advantage of them while they last.

**Makes 9.5 litres/2 gallons/2.4 US gallons**

24 elderflower heads

2 lemons

1.3kg/3lb/scant 7 cups granulated white sugar

30ml/2 tbsp white wine vinegar

9 litres/2 gallons/2.4 US gallons water

**Cook's Tips**
• Collect the elderflowers in full sunshine as this means the flavour will be at its most intense.
• This drink will keep in airtight bottles for a month or so.
• If you can't find elderflowers, or it isn't the right season for them, you can use elderflower cordial, which is available in some health food stores and other specialist outlets.

**1** Find a clean bucket that you can cover with a clean cloth. Put all the ingredients into it.

**2** Cover the bucket with a plastic sheet and leave overnight.

**3** Strain the elderflower drink then pour into bottles, leaving a space of about 2.5cm/1in at the top.

**4** Leave sealed for about 2 weeks in a cool place. A fermentation takes place and the result is a delightful, sparkling, refreshing, non-alcoholic drink.

Per batch Energy 1282kcal/5467kJ; Protein 1.7g; Carbohydrate 339.8g, of which sugars 339.8g; Fat 0g, of which saturates 0g; Cholesterol 0mg; Calcium 173mg; Fibre 0g; Sodium 20mg.

# Cranachan smoothie

Although a steaming bowl of porridge can't be beaten as a winter warmer, this sumptuous smoothie makes a great, light alternative in warmer months. Just a spoonful or so of rolled oats gives substance to this tangy, invigorating drink.

**Makes 1 large glass**

25ml/1½ tbsp medium rolled oats

150g/5oz/scant 1 cup raspberries

5–10ml/1–2 tsp clear honey

45ml/3 tbsp natural (plain) yogurt

**1** Put the rolled oats in a heatproof bowl. Pour in 120ml/4fl oz/½ cup boiling water and leave to stand in a warm place for about 10 minutes.

**2** Put the soaked oats in a food processor or blender and add all but two or three of the raspberries. Reserve the raspberries for decoration.

**3** Add the honey and about 30ml/ 2 tbsp of the yogurt to the food processor or blender. Purée the ingredients until smooth, scraping down the side of the bowl halfway through if necessary.

**4** Pour the raspberry and oat smoothie into a large glass, swirl in the remaining yogurt and top with the reserved raspberries.

**Cook's Tips**
• If you don't like raspberry pips (seeds) in your smoothies, press the fruit through a sieve to make a smooth purée, then process with the rolled oats and yogurt as above.
• If you can, prepare it ahead of time because soaking the raw oats helps to break down the starch into natural sugars that are easy to digest. The smoothie will thicken up in the refrigerator so you might need to stir in a little extra juice or mineral water just before serving.

**Per portion** Energy 186kcal/793kJ; Protein 7.5g; Carbohydrate 34.6g, of which sugars 16.4g; Fat 3.1g, of which saturates 0.4g; Cholesterol 1mg; Calcium 137mg; Fibre 5.5g; Sodium 51mg.

# Highland coffee

A good Highland coffee should be served in a tall wine glass with a 300ml/½ pint/1¼ cup capacity. The coffee should be freshly made and very hot. The whisky needs to be a Highland or Island malt, such as Dalwhinnie or Laphroaig.

**1** Pour the whisky into the glass and add the sugar. Stir thoroughly.

**2** Make a pot of fresh coffee and whilst it is still piping hot pour it into the glass with the whisky and sugar. Stand a spoon in the glass to stop it from cracking. Leave about 2cm/¾in at the top, and stir to dissolve the sugar.

**Serves 1**

30ml/2 tbsp malt whisky

5ml/1 tsp soft light brown sugar

hot black coffee

50ml/2fl oz/¼ cup double (heavy) cream, lightly whipped

**Cook's Tips**

• If the cream doesn't float well on top of the coffee, then the balance of coffee and sugar is not correct. Add a little bit more sugar, which will make the coffee more dense and the cream more likely to float.

• Use filter coffee or coffee made in a cafetière (press pot) for the best results.

**3** Using a teaspoon with its tip just touching the coffee gently pour the lightly whipped cream over the coffee until it reaches the top of the glass. Serve immediately.

**Per portion** Energy 83kcal/341kJ; Protein 0.2g; Carbohydrate 1.3g, of which sugars 1.3g; Fat 6.7g, of which saturates 4.2g; Cholesterol 17mg; Calcium 7mg; Fibre 0g; Sodium 3mg.

# Het pint

Meaning "hot pint" this is traditionally drunk at Hogmanay, with vendors in the street calling out to punters to try some. It is ideal for the night-long festivities, being both warming and sustaining with the addition of eggs which also provides a rich texture.

**Makes about 3 litres/5 pints**

1.2 litres/2 pints/5 cups lemonade

1.2 litres/2 pints/5 cups dark beer

5ml/1 tsp ground nutmeg

75g/3oz/⅓ cup caster (superfine) sugar

3 eggs

300ml/½ pint/1¼ cups whisky

**3** Whisk the eggs in a bowl and very slowly, while still beating, pour in a couple of ladlefuls of the hot mixture.

**4** Gently return the egg mixture to the main pan, whisking to make sure it does not form lumps or curdle by getting too hot around the edges.

**5** Add the whisky slowly, stirring continuously, and heat though to just below boiling point. Serve immediately by ladling the liquid into pint glasses (or tall glasses if you prefer) until it reaches the top. Hand it round to all the company and drink a hearty toast to Hogmanay.

**1** Put the lemonade and beer into a large heavy pan over a low heat.

**2** Add the nutmeg and heat gently to just below boiling point. Add the sugar and stir to dissolve.

**Cook's Tip**
This drink will only keep for a day or so, and it is better to drink it piping hot as soon as it's made. If you do want to store it, keep it in an airtight bottle.

**Per portion** Energy 425kcal/1888kJ; Protein 5.7g; Carbohydrate 43.6g, of which sugars 43.6g; Fat 4.2g, of which saturates 1.2g; Cholesterol 143mg; Calcium 70mg; Fibre 0g; Sodium 93mg.

# Index

# NOTES

# NOTES

# Notes

# NOTES